## *Rachel Had Never Felt Such Passion in a Kiss.*

At first stunned, she slowly succumbed, winding her arms around his neck, kissing him with impatient passion, lost in her own reactions.

She knew he wouldn't stop. When Jason twisted his body half onto the ground and pulled Rachel close against his side, she understood the message he was sending her. She felt him take a deep breath. Then he buried his face in her neck, kissing her hair.

"Oh, Maria," he moaned. "Maria . . ."

Rachel jerked away, her hands shaking. She was furious that she hadn't understood what was going on in his mind. To Jason Wilder, she wasn't a real woman—she was a character from his novel!

---

**BROOKE HASTINGS**

is that rare individual who can combine many careers and excel in all of them. In addition to her writing she is active in California politics and community affairs, and maintains a home for her husband of fourteen years and their two children.

Dear Reader,

Silhouette Special Editions are an exciting new line of contemporary romances from Silhouette Books. Special Editions are written specifically for our readers who want a story with heightened romantic tension.

Special Editions have all the elements you've enjoyed in Silhouette Romances and *more*. These stories concentrate on romance in a longer, more realistic and sophisticated way, and they feature greater sensual detail.

I hope you enjoy this book and all the wonderful romances from Silhouette. We welcome any suggestions or comments and invite you to write to us at the address below.

Karen Solem
Editor-in-Chief
Silhouette Books
P.O. Box 769
New York, N. Y. 10019

# BROOKE HASTINGS
## Intimate Strangers

*Silhouette Special Edition*
Published by Silhouette Books New York
America's Publisher of Contemporary Romance

**Other Silhouette Books by Brooke Hastings**

*Playing for Keeps*
*Innocent Fire*
*Desert Fire*
*Island Conquest*
*Winner Take All*

SILHOUETTE BOOKS, a Simon & Schuster Division of
GULF & WESTERN CORPORATION
1230 Avenue of the Americas, New York, N.Y. 10020

Distributed by Pocket Books

ISBN: 0-671-53502-1

First Silhouette Books printing February, 1982

10 9 8 7 6 5 4 3 2 1

Map by Tony Ferrara

SILHOUETTE, SILHOUETTE SPECIAL EDITION
and colophon are trademarks of Simon & Schuster.

America's Publisher of Contemporary Romance

Printed in the U.S.A.

*For Tasha, who told*
*me about Santandia*

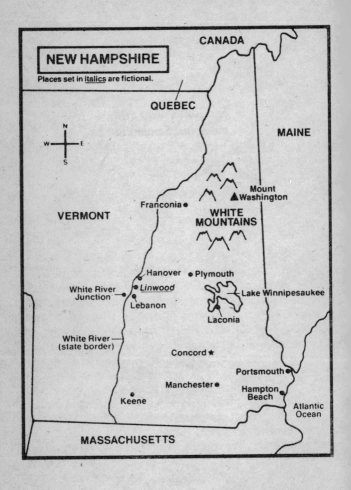

# Chapter One

From the Victorian Era to the 1980s, from Chinese diplomatic banquets to intimate New York dinner parties, haute cuisine has been associated with elegance and glamor; two qualities which are totally absent from the painstaking reality of its preparation. Rachel Grant and her younger sister, Susan Grant Lenglen, had from time to time endured the prattle of society matrons who allegedly envied them their catering business and who mused aloud about what fun it would be to own a funky little Manhattan restaurant where they would cook and serve their special Italian chicken, which everyone adored. No doubt they pictured themselves looking crisp and efficient, pristine chef's toques atop their carefully windblown coiffures, delivering orders with no-nonsense precision.

The reality of the catering business had nothing in

common with such fantasies except that the dishes in question were beautiful to look at and a delight to taste. On this late July evening, for example, the kitchen where the sisters worked was some ten to fifteen degrees hotter than the rest of the house: central air conditioning had failed to dissipate the heat produced by the two ovens and the six-burner range. Rachel, twenty-eight, and Susan, twenty-six, were dressed in sneakers, denim cut-offs and tank tops, the stains on their clothing bearing witness to an afternoon of cooking. Their work was physically demanding, and each of them had developed a strength and stamina at odds with the slenderness of her body. Even so, at the end of this flawless five-course dinner for sixteen, both would be exhausted.

They were taking a break between courses, sitting on oak kitchen stools and drinking iced tea, when the evening's employer made one of her sporadic appearances.

"Everything is perfectly exquisite. The ambassador and his wife are enchanted." Jacqueline Pollock flashed a smile almost as dazzling as the diamond clips in her upswept, silver-blond hair. With her throaty voice and calculatedly vulnerable gaze, dressed in a one-shouldered gown of black silk crepe de chine, Jacqueline Pollock seemed every inch the former model she was, and totally out of place in a kitchen. She seemed impervious to the heat which had coated the sisters' skins with a film of perspiration, her immunity perhaps perfected during long sessions under glaring klieg lights.

Rachel and Susan exchanged an amused look so subtle that it would have been indiscernible to anyone watching them. Both were thinking that one didn't dare present anything *less* than perfection when catering a dinner party for one of the chief lionesses in New York City's social pride.

"My guests have absolutely attacked the hors d'oeuvres," Mrs. Pollock went on. "Heaven knows how they'll manage the rest of it, but if the food is as marvelous as those little turnovers . . ." She paused, broadcasting a regal certainty that one of the sisters would provide her with the name of the dish.

*"Empadhinas."* Susan told her the correct Portuguese term.

"Yes, of course." She adjusted the lace rosette on the shoulder of her designer gown. "We'll be sitting down in the dining room in fifteen minutes. Richards will be in for the soup." She floated back out of the kitchen, a pair of smoked-glass sliding doors automatically parting as she approached and then shutting noiselessly once she had passed through.

Rachel watched the doors glide shut, then remarked, "Every time those doors open or close, I feel like I'm on the set of some way-out space movie."

"This place wasn't featured in that architectural magazine for nothing," Susan pointed out. "It would have been worth doing this job at cost just to work in the Pollocks' kitchen,"

"It *is* beautiful," Rachel agreed, "but somehow it lacks character." They exchanged a simultaneous smile, so in tune with each other that they might have been identical twins rather than merely sisters. Both were remembering the tribulations of their previous job, a buffet luncheon for thirty. Their ancient, erratic employer had required them to coax perfect souffles out of an equally ancient, equally erratic oven. In comparison to Iphigene Lambert, even the exacting Jacqueline Pollock had been a delight to work for.

This late in the summer, New York's heat and humidity had driven most of Susan and Rachel's regular customers out of the city and into Long Island beach cottages or upstate cabins. The two sisters had refused all bookings from mid-July until Labor Day, having made plans for their first vacations in four years. But one did not ignore an S.O.S. from Jacqueline Pollock and stay in business.

Mrs. Pollock had been one of New York's Beautiful People long before the term was invented, ever since her days as a leading haute couture model. The daughter of a California banking family, she was married to impresario Harold Pollock, a man whose extraordinary track record as a producer complemented his wife's wealth. When the couple's treasured French chef had been seduced back to Paris by a four-star restaurant, Mrs. Pollock had remembered an earlier dinner party catered by Susan and Rachel and picked up her telephone.

The guests of honor were to be the ambassador from the Court of St. James and his wife, she had explained in a self-important tone. Lady Caldecott, was, of course, a cousin of the royal family. Rachel might have been suitably intimidated by such well-connected specimens but for her own background as a diplomat's daughter. In fact, she had met Lord and Lady Caldecott some six years ago when they were stationed in the Latin American country of Santandia, as her own father had been.

There was no chance that she would meet them again this evening—she and Susan were hired to cook, not to mingle with the guests—but even if she did, she doubted that either of them would recognize her. She had looked older and harder as a twenty-two-year-old social butterfly than she did now, at twenty-eight. Six years ago, her blondish-red hair had been cut into a sleek, head-hugging style, artificial streaks accentuating the golden highlights. She had never set foot out of her father's house without first applying a heavy, professional-looking coat of makeup, and had worn nothing but soft, frilly dresses which now made her wince. When she looked at pictures from those days she thought that she resembled a soignee fashion doll. Certainly she had acted like one.

Rachel had lived through events that were painful, dramatic and even bizarre during the intervening six years, but regretted none of it. She knew several other women, including her own sister, who had endured as much anguish as she. The important thing was that she had changed. At twenty-two she had been a shallow child; now she was a woman, capable of empathy, proud of her accomplishments, respected by those she met. If a certain wary reserve had replaced her former empty vivacity she considered it an improvement.

She no longer buried her features under layers of cosmetics or spent hours each day shopping and visiting. She had rejected the padded bras she had once considered essential, and since she was slim and small-breasted, now looked natural rather than provocative. Her thick, straight hair was back to its natural color and had grown out to shoulder length. When she worked, she braided it into a single plait and pinned it into a loop to keep it out of her way. As for her wardrobe, she felt more comfortable in faded blue jeans than in silk prints these days.

Rachel's sister Susan privately thought that she was far more arresting at twenty-eight than she had been at eighteen. Her deep blue eyes, high cheekbones and firm, slightly full mouth hadn't changed, but tragedy had etched composure and dignity into her face. Though the first signs of aging had yet to appear, people seemed to sense her maturity and respect her need for privacy. However charmingly Rachel smiled, her controlled, authoritative manner and her talent for the most daunting sort of eye contact put even arrogant New York wolves on notice. Rachel was fully capable of pouring hollandaise sauce over the head of any man who got out of line and indeed, had done so on one memorable occasion.

Susan had started Grant Catering just over four years earlier, during the same June week that Rachel had moved to New York from Latin America. Because of her curly blond hair, soft green eyes, and small, curvy stature, she felt that she lacked Rachel's physical presence. Her insecurity translated itself into an inability to deal with her wealthy clientele. Afraid of giving offense, her impulse was to compromise or even to give way entirely.

As a result, Susan's customers had routinely taken advantage of her. They bargained her down on already-low prices, talked her into menus she disliked and intimidated her into feeling that she should pay *them* for the singular honor of catering their parties. She had gained a good deal of strength and self-confidence in the last few years, a result of coping with painful marital problems and her current separation from her husband, a physician. But even so, she would never have had the audacity to insist, as Rachel had, that Latin American food should be served at tonight's dinner party. Everyone knew that French cuisine was a Pollock trademark.

The "Richards" Mrs. Pollock had mentioned was a full-time retainer who appeared to fill a variety of roles in the household. A handsome man in his mid-twenties, he looked dashing in the waiter's uniform he wore tonight. He returned to the kitchen with several silver serving platters stacked in his arms, the remains of the appetizers consolidated on the top tray. There were *acarajes*, Brazilian fritters made from black-eyed peas, shrimp and onion, and served with a spicy sauce; *patacones*, green plantain chips from Colombia; and the turnovers Mrs. Pollock had praised, which were filled with either a cheese, shrimp or chopped beef mixture.

The next course was a chilled avocado soup which Rachel removed from the refrigerator and ladled into bowls. Susan then garnished each serving with fresh chopped coriander, or *cilantro*, as the herb was called in Latin America. Because they used only the freshest ingredients and pre-tested and refined all their recipes, the sisters had come to expect subtlety and excellence of themselves. Nonetheless, they appreciated the compliments that invariably reached them from the dining room.

The main course was roast duck, garnished with a sauce made of allspice, hot peppers, cloves, cinnamon and wine, among other ingredients. *Arroz con coco y pasas*—rice with coconut and raisins—would accompany the duck, with a tossed green salad to follow. The dessert was a Mexican coconut custard called *cocada*, which was chilled and garnished with slivered almonds.

Between courses, Richards sat on a kitchen stool and watched Rachel and Susan work, eating his own meal and talking about the guests while one of them corrected a sauce or arranged food on a platter. In addition to Lord and Lady Caldecott, tonight's guest list included a prima ballerina who danced with a leading New York company; a former secretary of state and his professor wife; a knighted British archaelogist and his American wife, who, Richards informed them, by now sounded even more properly British than her husband; and several prominent businessmen. Finally, Jacqueline Pollock's younger sister, Paula Chapin, and her playwright-husband Stephen were present. Rachel had seen several of Stephen Chapin's plays and admired his work. She had heard that the man had a reputation for plain speaking which bordered on rudeness, but if Paula Chapin were half as assertive as her sister, she could no doubt cope with *that*.

"Your run-of-the-mill New York crew," Rachel observed with studied nonchalance. "Smart, successful, and—" she broke into a smile, "absolutely gluttonous, thank heaven."

"They couldn't say no to Jacqueline Pollock any more than we could," Susan added with a laugh, "even though I'll bet most of them would rather be out of town in this heat."

A light flashed over the doorway, indicating that their hostess was ready for the next course. By the time the guests retired to the living room for after-dinner drinks and more conversation, Susan and Rachel had slumped into two contoured modern chairs in the breakfast room adjacent to the kitchen.

The automatic doors slid open to reveal Mrs.

Pollock, who glided up to the dinette table. Susan and Rachel automatically started to pull themselves to their feet, gratefully obeying their employer's gesture for them to remain seated.

"You were quite right, Rachel," she said with a smile. "The ambassador confided that he's adored Latin American food ever since his tour of duty in Santandia." Her eyes flicked to Susan, implicitly including her in the next statement even though they immediately returned to Rachel. "Come work for me. With Marcel off to Paris, I'll need a replacement."

"I'm sorry, Mrs. Pollock." Susan started to answer only when she realized that Rachel had no intention of doing so. "We appreciate the compliment, but we enjoy free-lancing."

"Nonesense! I'll pay you twenty percent more than you earned last year, and for working far less hard. You'll be cooking for people who appreciate fine food. And where," she added, her hand sweeping dramatically behind her in the approximate direction of the ovens, "could you find such magnificent facilities?"

Rachel caught Susan's helpless look. She had wanted her sister to issue the refusal for once, but supposed that Jacqueline Pollock was the wrong person to start with. "Your offer isn't the first one we've received, and although it's a tempting one, we'll have to decline, Mrs. Pollock." Rachel used a pleasant but firm tone. "It's been a pleasure working with you, though, and we hope you'll call us again when you need our help."

Mrs. Pollock paused before replying, the assumed vulnerability in her eyes briefly replaced by annoyance. Then she smiled as if crestfallen and said, "I'm disappointed, of course, but I *do* understand. And thank you for coming. When you're ready to leave, Richards will drive you home."

When the sliding glass doors had glided closed, Susan shook her head, bewilderment coloring the admiration on her face. "I don't know how you do it. She was actually afraid of pressing you. As if offending us could make the slightest difference to someone in her position."

"The trick is to convince her that it does," Rachel drawled, "even though five minutes from now she'll probably wonder why she took 'no' for an answer."

Even though Rachel and Susan were paid solely to cook, they stayed to help Richards clean up the kitchen. Then they gathered up their own spices, molds, pots and tools, carefully repacking everything into cardboard cartons. Fortunately, the Pollocks' kitchen was unusually well equipped, so they had had to bring relatively few extras with them today. Afterwards, they accepted Richards' invitation to unwind over a glass of wine and sat down in the breakfast room with him, telling him about previous jobs.

When Jacqueline Pollock came back into the kitchen, Rachel thought to herself that her earlier words to Susan had been prophetic. After all, the lady had a reputation for persistence. She would have to refuse more firmly this time.

But their employer's voice was amused rather than peremptory when she stated the reason for her reappearance. "One of my guests is determined to speak with you. She needs a cook until Labor Day. I told her that you had had the effrontery to turn even *me* down"—she smiled, no longer offended—"but

Livie insisted on talking to you herself. I'll warn you now, she has a talent for getting her own way."

"Mrs. Pollock, we're hardly dressed . . ." Susan began, self-consciously adjusting the strap of her tank top.

"Don't be silly, dear. You look charmingly bedraggled. We'll be in the den—straight through the dining room, right into the hall, and back to the last room on the left. But do finish your wine first." She turned on her heel, permitting no argument, and sailed out of the room. Richards, a broad grin on his face, tactfully excused himself so that the two sisters could talk over the offer.

"Stop worrying," Rachel said, laughing at the concerned frown on Susan's face. "No one's going to talk us into anything."

"Maybe not you . . ."

"I'll do the talking. You're going to Europe with Sarah on Monday even if I have to push you onto the plane myself. It's been a very tough year and a half for you, and you need to have some fun."

Susan sipped her wine, unsuccessfully trying to hide her uncertainty. "What about you? Between school and the business, you haven't had a single free week since Carlos—" she interrupted herself, "since you came to New York. Why won't you come along with us?"

"I've told you, Suzy, I promised myself I was going to spend August catching up on plays and museums, not traipsing through ruins." Rachel pretended not to have noticed her sister's inadvertent reference to Carlos Garcia Martinez, her late husband. "Besides, I want to do some writing. I'm late with that article for *Homemaker Magazine,* and I might even try some fiction if I can find the time."

Susan shrugged. "Then let's get it over with. Whoever 'Livie' is, she can't possibly be worse than Jacqueline Pollock."

They followed Mrs. Pollock's directions to a mahogany door, slightly ajar. An exasperated male voice drifted out into the hallway where they stood waiting.

". . . And he knows I wrote it for him, damn him, but he won't budge. Work on him for me. You're the only person who can talk him into anything."

"You overestimate my powers of persuasion, Stephen darling." The speaker was apparently the "Livie" they were about to confront. Judging by the English accent to her lilting speech, she must be the archaeologist's wife. What did she need a cook for? Rachel wondered. A dig in Egypt?

"I'll do my best, of course," she continued. "Your play sounds perfect for him, but I very much doubt I'll have any more luck than you did. You know why he refuses to consider acting again."

Rachel took advantage of a pause in the conversation to knock on the door and was immediately invited into a masculine, wood-paneled den. The male speaker, whom she recognized as playwright Stephen Chapin, immediately got up and stalked out of the room. He gave no indication of even noticing Rachel or Susan.

The woman seated next to Jacqueline Pollock on the wine-colored leather couch looked incongruous amidst the substantial furniture and dark color scheme of the room. She was wearing a halter-topped blue gown which set off her porcelain complexion and light blue eyes to perfection. Her blond hair was piled atop her head with little curls pulled out to frame her face, a style which gave an impression of intense femininity. Rachel judged her to be in her late forties.

"Livie darling, these are the wizards who conjured up our wonderful dinner tonight, Rachel Grant and her sister, Susan Lenglen. Ladies, this is my very dear friend, Olivia, Lady Ronald Bennett, who, as I've warned you, is far more persuasive than I. And the impossibly rude man who failed to wait for an introduction was my brother-in-law, Stephen Chapin. We only tolerate him because he's a genius."

Lady Bennett reached forward and extended her hand across the coffee table, her smile radiant. "I'm so pleased to meet you both. Do sit down, you look exhausted. Delightful dinner—so unusual. It's an absolute stroke of luck that Ronny and I were able to be here tonight. We might have left town, you know. But of course, Jackie asked us to stay. Charles and Betsy are such dear friends."

Rachel and Susan shook her hand and seated themselves in two wing chairs, Susan looking bemused, Rachel self-possessed. She knew that "Charles and Betsy" were the ambassador and his wife; as for "Ronny," he must be Lady Bennett's husband. Jacqueline Pollock slipped out of the room and shut the door behind her, leaving them to Lady Ronald Bennett's mercy.

"I expect Jackie told you my problem," she went on. "You see, Ronny—my husband—is going off on one of his digs on Friday. He's really much too old to tramp through the jungle swinging a ridiculous machete, but it's a question of some buried city. Well, there's certainly no point in my going home and brooding about it, is there?"

Rachel and Susan solemnly shook their heads,

even though neither had the remotest notion of what Lady Bennett was leading up to.

"Exactly," she stated with satisfaction. "So I've decided to stay in America for a month or so, but New York simply won't do. Far too hot and humid. My son lives in New Hampshire. Shuts himself up in the attic of a marvelous old Georgian house he moved all the way from Portsmouth and writes all day and half the night. I've told him I'm coming to visit, but I have no intention of living like a hermit. He's very poor company, after all, and besides, one wants to visit with one's friends, doesn't one? Entertaining properly is so important, don't you agree?" She paused, then directed a beatific smile at her quarry.

"I'll be in Europe with a friend," Susan answered, relieved that Lady Bennett's primary target appeared to be Rachel. That was nothing unusual, however. Customers instinctively directed their questions to her sister.

"How very disappointing," Lady Bennett said, sounding crushed. Then she brightened. "But I'm certain Miss Grant will manage very well on her own, won't you, dear?"

Miss Grant's customary reserve was giving way in the face of her adversary's dotty charm. It was impossible not to be amused by Olivia Bennett, whose outwardly flighty manner obviously masked the strength of will of a wolverine.

"I'm afraid I'll have to disappoint you also," she said. "I'm staying in New York for the rest of the summer."

"Then you have no special plans?" Lady Bennett asked.

Rachel shook her head. "Only to do exactly as I

please, Lady Bennett. I'm flattered by your invitation, but I can't possibly accept."

"A few weeks, then," Lady Bennett coaxed. "Do reconsider, Miss Grant. It's lovely in New Hampshire this time of year, far more livable than New York. Think of it as a vacation. Cook a few meals now and again and the rest of your time will be your own. Swimming, tennis, horseback riding, sunbathing . . ."

The prospect was tempting, but Rachel knew enough of such arrangements to realize that a "few meals" could easily mean four a day, including high tea. She was about to repeat her demurral when Lady Bennett went on, "Just promise me you'll think about it. I assure you that you'll never see my son—he's up in that attic of his all the time. And *we'll* get along splendidly. I'll be in town through the end of the week."

Rachel had long ago learned that dishonesty was sometimes necessary with the Olivia Bennetts of this world. "I'll certainly do that," she said, knowing that she had no intention of going up to New Hampshire, no matter how amused she was by the lady's off-beat manner. "If I change my mind, I'll call you."

"Marvelous. I'm staying with Jackie, naturally." Lady Bennett rose from the leather couch with a graceful economy of movement and Rachel was surprised to find that she was slightly taller than her own five-foot-five. Seated, she had given an impression of petite fragility. They walked out of the room together, Rachel admiring the way Lady Bennett carried herself. She moved like a model or a dancer.

Rachel and Susan returned to the kitchen to find that Richards had already loaded their cartons and was ready to drive them home. They accompanied him down to the street and into the Pollocks' black limousine, which was parked at the curb. There was very little traffic this late at night, and the trip across Central Park to their West Side apartment took less than fifteen minutes.

Rachel immediately clicked on the air conditioner in the bedroom. It emitted a series of distressing clangs, prompting her to hastily shut it off and open a window. "I think we'll have to buy a new one," she said to Susan. "We'd be wasting our money to have it fixed again." She smiled wearily. "Maybe New Hampshire isn't such a bad idea. I kind of like Lady Bennett. And it *is* a lot cooler up there."

She was talking off the top of her head, not at all serious about changing her plans. Susan, she suddenly realized, looked tense, her face oddly pinched. "Is there something the matter?" Rachel asked her.

"You don't want to go up to New Hampshire," Susan said, taking an uncharacteristic interest in the broken machinery.

Rachel cocked her head, puzzled by her sister's unusual evasiveness. "Stop fiddling with that thing, Suzy; you know you can barely change a lightbulb. Tell me why I shouldn't go to New Hampshire."

"Because you had other plans, Rachel. You'd be bored up there—it's too quiet for you. And you know we never work for people, I mean, not like that, not full time."

"You're a terrible liar, Susan," Rachel informed her sister. "Stop trying to stonewall me—you know you're rotten at it."

Susan abandoned the air conditioner and began to undress, saying nothing. Rachel forced herself to patiently do the same. Only when both of them had washed up and climbed into bed did Rachel again prompt, "Susan?"

Susan clicked off the lamp that sat on the night-table between the twin beds. "I read an article about the Bennetts the other day," she said. "Did you know that Sir Ronald is Lady Bennett's second husband?"

"How utterly fascinating," Rachel drawled. "Is this leading anywhere, Susan?"

"All right, yes," Susan blurted out. "Her first husband was named Julian Wilder. He was a lawyer from an old New England family. That son she mentioned—the writer who shuts himself up in his attic—"

"Is Jason Wilder," Rachel interrupted. "That's quite a coincidence." Her ironic tone effectively concealed the painfully mixed emotions she felt.

Jason Wilder was not quite the hermit his mother made him out to be. He occasionally came to New York, where he moved in the same social circle as Rachel and Susan's clientele. Rachel had fantasized about meeting him, daydreams that began with a torrent of bitter words, and, to her mortification, somehow managed to end in passionate lovemaking. Faced with the prospect of finally confronting him, however, her anger and pain far outweighed any fascination he held for her.

She had good reason to dislike him. He had taken her most personal thoughts and feelings, emotions so intensely painful and private that not even her family spoke openly about them, and splattered them all over the printed page for millions of strangers to wallow in. Although the book based on her life, *A Latin American Tragedy,* had come out over a year ago, Rachel continued to be distressed by it.

She knew only as much about the author as the rest of the world. Classically trained, he had started his career as a stage actor, working on both coasts, and had been selected to star in the movie *Parallel Universe* while working in Los Angeles. The film, enormously successful, had made him an international star; its two sequels had made him wealthy.

Even on a movie screen, with the camera magnifying every flaw, Jason Wilder was a magnetically handsome man. His directors, no doubt mindful of his female fans, had often contrived to photograph him with a minimum of clothing on his lean body. Rachel could picture his six-foot frame with its smooth, powerful chest, sturdy legs, and strong, muscled arms. His thatch of dirty blond hair, light blue eyes and cleft chin made him look boyish no matter how expert his delivery of jaded frowns and sardonic smiles. He resembled the quintessential all-American hero, and the world-weary cynicism of the character he played fooled no one in the audience. His appearance eternally proclaimed that he was on the side of the angels. Although his fans loved to think of him as tough and just a little bit dangerous, they refused to accept him as anything other than a good guy, and none of his other movies had captivated the public in quite the same way as the *Parallel Universe* trilogy.

Along with the money and fame the role brought him, Jason Wilder had acquired a beautiful wife, television actress Meredith Lloyd. Three years after their marriage, she had been found dead in another man's bed, the coroner ruling that she was the victim of an accidental overdose of tranquilizers mixed with liquor.

Jason Wilder had never made another movie, turning to print as a means of expressing himself. He gave interviews only when some enterprising journalist cornered him on one of his trips to New York and was customarily flip, obscure or irreverent when he deigned to talk to the media. He refused to discuss any aspect of his private life and was no more illuminating when it came to his books. He could be charming and amusing on any number of topics, but preferred, he insisted, to let his novels speak for themselves.

Much to Susan's distress, Rachel went out of her way to watch his brief television appearances, to read every interview and every item of gossip about him. Susan had once accused Rachel of being obsessed with the man and Rachel knew there was an element of truth in the charge. As much as she disliked Jason Wilder, she couldn't help being fascinated by him.

His first novel, *Tinseltown,* had been published three years earlier, when he was thirty-four. It was generally considered to be autobiographical, an often lurid, compelling story of life in Hollywood, its tense, gripping tone relieved by mordantly witty humor. The two main characters were a director and his actress-wife, both of them eventually destroyed by the husband's compulsiveness and jealousy. Given the author's celebrity status, it wasn't surprising that *Tinseltown* had become an immediate bestseller. .

Wilder's second novel, *A Latin American Tragedy,* had come out the previous July. Beyond Rachel's justifiable anger over the way the book had used her as source material, she was haunted by the thought that someone she had never met could know so much about her—more, in fact, than anyone in the world. The book had hit much closer to the mark than even her family realized. She wasn't about to demean herself by writing to her so-called friends in Santandia to find out how many of them had talked to Jason Wilder, but it had to be more than a few. The man wrote from the gut. He had felt and understood every emotion before putting it down on paper.

Rachel's parents and sister had begged her not to read *A Latin American Tragedy,* but she hadn't listened to them. The novel had been much too widely reviewed and discussed to ignore. On more than one occasion she had sat in the same room with would-be critics and listened to them tear apart the character of Maria—tear *her* apart—and said nothing. Only briefly had she considered a lawsuit. The book was probably too accurate to be libelous, and in any event, there was no way she could face reliving her marriage and her husband's subsequent kidnapping and death in court. In the first few months after the novel was published the thought of even seeing Jason Wilder was enough to make Rachel tremble with anxiety, and with a self-hatred so strong that she was plunged into a depression about the girl she had once been, the Maria of the book.

Now Rachel wished Susan good-night, but it was hours before she slept. The irony of her intense reaction to a man she had never met was not lost on her. During her marriage to Carlos Garcia Martinez she had learned not to feel, not to be affected by his veiled sarcasm and condescension. And after his kidnapping, with the press hounding her, she had learned to cope with crassness and inadvertent cruelty by retreating behind a composed façade which by now was genuine rather than feigned. Although she enjoyed male company, she let no man breech the shell she had erected around herself. The caring, giving side of her nature was reserved for Susan and a few close friends.

She assumed that, his screen persona to the contrary, Jason Wilder was totally heartless in reality. Hadn't he admitted as much in *Tinseltown?* And if he had had any decency, would he have written *A Latin American Tragedy,* thoughtlessly invading her privacy?

If Rachel's emotions were mixed it was only because honesty compelled her to acknowledge the sensitivity of the latter work, and the fact that Jason Wilder had disdained Maria precisely because he saw the potential she was too shallow and vain to exploit. Rachel had struggled hard to achieve her present maturity, and yet on some level, she felt that only Jason Wilder could validate that growth, because only he would truly understand how far she had come. She hated his knowledge of her . . . and craved his approval.

At that moment, however, knowing that she would finally meet him, she could think only of the torment his book had inflicted. Fate had provided the perfect opportunity to pay him back and she would take advantage of it. She would live in his house for the next month, gaining the confidence of servants, neighbors, family and tradesmen. She would find out everything there was to know about him and then write it up as a magazine article for everyone to read. And when it finally appeared, she told herself, she would have the satisfaction of knowing that Jason Wilder understood how it felt to have one's privacy forceably stripped away, one's most personal emotions paraded before the pandered-to public.

# *Chapter Two*

*R*achel woke to the aroma of chocolate cake, a delightful, if unreliable, alarm clock. In addition to catering any meal from a continental breakfast to a midnight supper, she and Susan provided desserts for a nearby Manhattan restaurant. They specialized in chocolate cakes, cheese pies and indecently moist French tortes and, had they had enough time and oven space, could easily have sold twice as many desserts as they did at present. The news that they were going on vacation had produced sighs of dismay from their customer, but their desserts were so excellent that he was willing to make alternate arrangements until Labor Day.

"I could gain five pounds just from inhaling," Rachel said as she poured herself some corn flakes. "What's cooking?"

"A pair of cakes from that chocolate dessert book

we were testing last month," Susan told her. "I phoned our restaurant this morning to let Andre know what we were sending over and he started begging me not to abandon him." She smiled. "Half in French and half in English. It tore at my heart, Rachel. Since you're going to stay in New York, maybe you could manage at least . . ."

"But I'm not." Rachel pushed aside her bowl of cereal, only too aware of what Susan was hinting at. Their relationship was too close to let them avoid the subject of Jason Wilder, but Rachel at least hoped to avoid an argument over him. "I've decided to go up to New Hampshire," she continued.

"Oh, no." Susan's voice, initially a breathless moan, strengthened as she told her sister, "You almost had a nervous breakdown because of that man, Rachel. You can't go up to New Hampshire— there's no point in putting yourself through the trauma of meeting him. What good can possibly come of it?"

Rachel shrugged, looking far more composed than she felt. "I'm a writer. He's a good subject."

Susan, obviously appalled by Rachel's train of thought, shook her head in dismay. She poured two cups of coffee and set one down in front of her sister. "I think you need a jolt of caffeine to wake you up, Rachel Grant. If you don't put that blasted book behind you it's going to haunt you for the rest of your life. You can take all the revenge you want, but it won't make you feel any better."

"*I* think it will," Rachel answered.

Susan sat down, her assertiveness beginning to wilt. Rachel was irrational on the subject of Jason Wilder. Perhaps a different sort of appeal would reach her. "If Wilder catches you, he'll kill you," she said. "You must realize that, Rachel."

"Don't be so dramatic. Anyway, he won't catch me—not until the article's in print."

"You can't really believe that! For heaven's sake, Rachel, he's going to know who you are the minute he meets you. You can't expect him not to be suspicious about why you're up there."

"Really?" Rachel, normally patient with her younger sister, permitted herself a withering stare. "I seem to remember that you once insisted that his novel wasn't based on my marriage alone—that it also dealt with Santandian high society in general. Why should he connect Rachel Grant with Raquel Garcia Martinez? I look very different now."

"Because Daddy was interviewed two or three times, both as the former American ambassador and as Carlos's father-in-law. Wilder must have come across the interviews in his research and he'll connect the names. And there were pictures of you in so many papers and magazines, Rachel. I admit you look different, and maybe he won't place you right away, but eventually he's going to put it together."

"So what if he does?" Rachel asked. Even if Susan were right, she had decided to go to New Hampshire and she wasn't changing her mind. She could handle Jason Wilder. "As far as he'll know, I'm up there to cook because his mother fell in love with my *empadhinas*. That's no more unbelievable than meeting Lady Bennett in the first place. To Jason Wilder, I'm a vapid little butterfly, Suzy. He doesn't know that I finished college or that I've had articles published. You think he's ever read a women's magazine in his life?"

Susan sighed, weary of an argument that had been hopeless from the start. Rachel had always been the more stubborn and determined of the two. Even though Susan was the one with years of formal training as a chef, her father had had to subsidize her income until Rachel's resolve and flair had turned Grant Catering into a reliable living for both of them. At least, she thought, she could try to instill some caution into her uncharacteristically reckless sister.

"Okay," she said at last. "Just do me a favor, Rachel. Please be careful. Don't provoke him. I don't think you should tangle with a man who . . ."

"For heaven's sake!" Rachel interrupted, her defensiveness finding its outlet in attack. "You're confusing the man's screen image with real life, Susan. This is the twentieth century. He may be nasty, but do you really think he's going to burst into my room some dark and stormy night with murder or rape in mind?"

Susan had been thinking of Wilder's barbed pen and sharp tongue, not his beautiful body, and the image evoked by Rachel's tirade was so ludicrous that she began to laugh. "He could burst into *my* room any time," she said, "provided he was dying to seduce me."

"Better him than no one!" Rachel snapped. The thoughtless remark wounded her sister, whose eyes were moist as she looked away. Rachel, disgusted with herself for letting her anger with Wilder express itself in cruelty to her sister, reached over and covered Susan's hand with her own.

"I'm sorry, Suzy. That was a terrible thing to say. I guess this whole thing's upset me more than I'll admit, and I took it out on you. A lot of what you say is true, and maybe I'm acting irrationally, but I'm going through with this anyway. I *have* to meet him."

"At least you can make decisions, even if they're crazy ones," Susan murmured. "I don't seem to be able to do anything. I don't go out with other guys and I don't file for divorce. I take Philip's phone calls, but I'm afraid of seeing him when he comes back to New York. He'll be finished at Boston Children's next month and he's talking about starting a private practice here. I have to do something one way or the other."

In Rachel's opinion Susan had a tendency to be much too hard on herself. Now she reminded her sister that she *could* make decisions when she had to. "You refused to give up the business when he ordered you to, even though it was hard for you to stand up to him. If he was so insecure that having a wife with a life of her own made him go out and have an affair, that's *his* problem. You had no choice but to leave, and you did."

"He wanted me to forgive him, to come back."

"On *his* terms," Rachel said gently. "He was married to his work, Suzy. What kind of life was it, with a husband who spent twenty-three hours a day either working or sleeping? The affair with that stupid little tramp isn't the problem—it's whether Philip is capable of putting some real effort into your relationship."

Susan looked up, so silently miserable that Rachel pulled over her chair and put an arm around her sister's shoulder, to comfort her. "I know you want him to be, Suzy," she said. "And there's nothing wrong with having waited a year and a half, not when you still love him. You know I think Philip has a lot going for him, but he has serious problems, too. You'll have to see what happens when he comes back. Maybe he'll be willing to try some marital counseling now."

Susan disengaged herself, rubbing her eyes. "I don't know what I would have done if it hadn't been for you, Rachel."

Rachel smiled. "I wasn't such a prize when I got back from Santandia." She sniffed the air. "Suzy, the cakes!"

Each of them ran for an oven, rescuing a chocolate cake from imminent disaster.

In the middle of the afternoon, Rachel phoned the Pollock residence and asked for Lady Bennett, only to be told by an amused Richards that she and Mrs. Pollock were out at a Wednesday matinee. Rachel left her telephone number, along with the message that Richards had obviously anticipated: she had decided to accept Lady Bennett's offer of a job. As she had expected, her call was returned that evening.

"I'm so pleased," Lady Bennett said without prelude. "Of course, I knew you would agree, Miss—oh, that's impossibly formal, dear. Your first name is Rachel, isn't it?"

"You have a good memory," Rachel said, realizing that it had probably never occurred to Lady Bennett that she wouldn't ultimately get her way. No doubt she had been prepared to cajole, blandish and wheedle until she tasted victory.

"It will be Rachel and Olivia, then," Lady Bennett announced. "I'm still an American, you know. Never gave up my citizenship. The title is quite meaningless here. Unconstitutional, I believe. Not that Ronny wasn't pleased, you understand, because the British always are. It's lovely to be recognized for one's contributions, and Ronny is utterly brilliant. He adores it."

Rachel, automatically transposing Lady Bennett's disjointed sentences into coherent thoughts, wondered how many people were taken in by her apparent flightiness. "I'd like to know more about your husband," she answered.

"Jason has all his books, dear. You'll have plenty of time to read them, I promise you."

"Jason is your son, I take it," Rachel remarked, pleased at how offhanded she sounded. "I'll look forward to borrowing them, then. I've never been to New Hampshire, Olivia. Is there a decent supermarket where your son lives?"

"It's quite in the middle of nowhere actually, Rachel. Near a town called Linwood. Jacqueline's butcher is packing everything up in dry ice; he's an absolute angel, so there's no need to worry."

Rachel took a moment to interpret this statement. Apparently Lady Bennett had arranged to bring along her own meat. Presumably, Rachel thought, Jason Wilder had someplace to store it. She was picturing a house surrounded by a virgin forest, with a walk-in meat locker powered by its own generator, when Lady Bennett corrected the image.

"He was simply furious when the freezer arrived, Rachel. I ordered it sent, you see, because he has one of those side-by-side models and I knew perfectly well that it wouldn't be large enough. He almost threw it out, but he knows I would merely have sent another if he had."

"Is his house accessible by car?" Rachel asked, shaking her head in wonderment. Whatever else she thought about Jason Wilder, he was obviously an indulgent son.

"I asked him to pick me up, but he refused. Couldn't spare the time, he said. He's obsessed with his wretched book just now. I told him the characters are more important to him than I am, but he simply laughed at me. And the plane just sits there, Rachel. Jacqueline is loaning us Richards. He'll drive us up."

"Your son has his own airplane?" Given his reclusive lifestyle, Rachel was surprised that he found much use for it.

"He enjoys flying," Lady Bennett explained, "and he loathes commercial flights. People are all over him, you see. He's never quite gotten used to that. The crowds make him uncomfortable."

If ever a statement were designed to set her up, Rachel thought, Lady Ronald Bennett had just made it. Her wacky non sequiturs to the contrary, she wanted to find out exactly how much Rachel knew.

There was no point in pretending ignorance. "To be honest, my sister warned me last night," she said in a voice indicating her disinterest in the subject. "She read an article about you and your husband and it mentioned your son. Frankly, Olivia, much as I look forward to spending some time in New Hampshire, your son has a reputation for having a very sharp tongue. If he starts using it on me, I'm going to leave."

It was apparently the right thing to say. Lady Bennett, suddenly as soothing as a mother cooing to her fussy baby, assured Rachel that Jason would be on his best behavior; she personally guaranteed it. Since the man obviously had a soft spot for his mother it was possible that he would curb his penchant for cutting wit. But Rachel doubted it.

Rachel and Susan spent Thursday cleaning and packing. There had been no further discussion about either Jason Wilder or Dr. Philip Lenglen, although the latter had phoned that morning to wish his wife a pleasant vacation. There was no doubt in Rachel's mind that he wanted Susan back because he called her several times a month. There had been no indication, however, that he was prepared to do anything differently if she agreed to return.

Rachel understood why her sister loved the man. He was an extremely gifted plastic surgeon and if he could have lavished even half the care and attention on his wife that he devoted to his patients there would have been no problem. She had seen him blink away tears when talking about some of his patients—children with horrible facial deformities who were desperate for the help he could provide. The problem was that he wouldn't let himself feel the same intense emotion toward those closest to him. He was afraid to love too much, and Rachel didn't understand why.

Susan and her friend Sarah would be flying to Paris Monday morning and Rachel hoped that the time off would give her sister the opportunity to think about the future. She had to put her marriage in perspective and decide whether a reconciliation was possible; living in limbo was slowly ripping her apart.

After lunch on Friday Rachel exhorted Susan to enjoy every minute of her trip to France, taking a copy of her sister's itinerary and promising to write to her care of general delivery. Then the two of them carried Rachel's bags down to the lobby and waited together for Lady Bennett to arrive.

At precisely two o'clock a garishly painted late model van pulled up in front of the apartment building. Richards—Rachel was never to learn his first name, if indeed he had one—hopped out of the driver's side, flashed a friendly smile at Rachel and Susan as they emerged from the building and opened up the back of the van. A moment later Rachel's two suitcases and small overnight bag joined the designer luggage already stowed there.

Lady Bennett had brought along four large cases and several smaller specialty pieces: a train case, hat box, and shoe carrier. Sitting on the floor next to this expensive leather luggage was a sizable wooden crate. The old cliché, "enough food to feed an army," came to Rachel's mind. Having talked to Lady Bennett twice now, it didn't surprise her that her employer had been free with her invitations; she only wondered how Jason Wilder would react to the upcoming invasion. Perhaps he would simply climb into his airplane and take off in the direction of Canada where he could perfect his latest hatchet job in peace.

Rachel had packed only one evening outfit, a jumpsuit made of a silklike synthetic. The same suitcase also contained jeans, sweaters, blouses and underwear, while the other held only cookbooks, hard-to-find spices and specialty cooking utensils. It was uncomfortably muggy and overcast in New York, so she had dressed in yellow shorts and a matching camisole top and carried an all-weather coat over her arm. Her hair was pulled back into a ponytail, which was held in place by a covered elastic band. With only a light coat of protective makeup on her face she looked nothing at all like the plastically-groomed Raquel Garcia Martinez.

Rachel greeted Lady Bennett with a cheerful, "Good afternoon, Olivia," kissed Susan good-bye and climbed into the van. Her employer was dressed in a safari-styled pants outfit, appropriate garb for the trek on which they were about to embark. The inside of the van was well-suited for long journeys, fitted out with a pair of leather-covered bucket seats in front, a card table between a pair of banquettes in the middle and thick carpeting throughout.

"It belongs to Jackie's son," Lady Bennett told Rachel as they sat down on opposite sides of the table. "He's a college student, and Harry Pollock told me he's been known to use the area in back for something other than the transportation of luggage. I can't imagine what he meant."

"It was nice of him to lend it to us," Rachel said, smiling at Lady Bennett's pretended naïveté. She reminded Rachel of her late paternal grandmother, an equally fragile-looking lady with a talent for slightly racy humor. Because of her innocent appearance, Nana's naughty puns had been twice as funny.

"He's off to the Pollocks' beach house with some of his friends. Co-ed, I don't doubt," Lady Bennett added. "Richards will take the van back tomorrow. I'm surprised *you're* not off to the beach, Rachel. You're very lovely. Did you learn to cook by taking lessons?"

"Thank you, Olivia." It was all Rachel could do not to laugh. This business of skipping around from subject to subject was rather unnerving and she could easily imagine someone like her sister attempting to reply to each of the last three sentences in turn.

Instead, she offered the information that Susan was the trained chef of the pair and continued with a non sequitur of her own. "I hope your son will let me drive his car, since we won't have the van."

"The last time I visited, he had a jeep. Ghastly thing. Rattled my teeth to drive around in it. So I've hired a car. They brought it yesterday." She paused, then smiled in that angelic way of hers. "I'm afraid it was no more popular than the freezer, Rachel. Do you ride?"

It took Rachel a moment to realize that Lady Bennett was referring to equines rather than automobiles. "Yes. Does your son keep horses?"

"Only one. His name is Caligula."

"Caligula?" Rachel repeated.

"From the Camus play rather than the historical emperor I should think. Do you know it?"

Rachel nodded. She had read the play in college. "But the character was an amoral monster. Why would your son name his horse after someone like that?"

"I really don't know. His sense of humor can be rather indecipherable at times, Rachel, but the fact is, the horse *is* a bit of a devil. Perhaps some company will calm him down. He has the loveliest barn."

"Company?" Rachel asked. "Don't tell me you had *horses* delivered, too?"

"Jason's language is not to be repeated, Rachel. Worse than in *Tinseltown*, until he remembered that his sainted mother was at the other end of the line. I have a friend who lives in Hanover, you see. She arranged the entire business—three horses, shipped right to Jason's house for the next month. How was I to know that one of the mares would come into

*40*

heat? Caligula was beside himself. I'm afraid the barn suffered a bit as a result, but it's quite all right now. We've procured a substitute."

Rachel shook her head, by now laughing openly. "What *else* did you send up there?"

"That was all really, unless you count my extra-firm mattress. Shall we play cards?"

They settled on casino and then gin, and although Rachel was a good card player Lady Bennett beat her two out of every three games. As they drove she told Rachel something of her own life. Her first husband had died when Jason was only ten and she had married Ronald Bennett two years later. They had had two children together, a son who was an archaeologist, like his father, and would be accompanying him to South America, and a daughter who was still a student. Given the fact that Jason Wilder was in his late thirties his mother had to be close to sixty, but she looked ten years younger. At one point in the conversation she casually mentioned that "Ronny" was five years her junior. In the 1950s, marrying a younger man had been far more daring than it was today and Rachel admired Lady Bennett's unconventionality.

Inevitably, the conversation turned to Rachel's background, and although she tried to limit her confidences to the last few years, Lady Bennett kept returning to the subject of her family. Rachel felt it would be a mistake to refuse comment—it would appear that she was hiding something, which of course she was. She settled on the vague statement that her father worked for the government, saying that she had lived in a number of foreign countries while growing up. Her interest in cooking had started with sessions in the kitchen supervised by the family's cooks, who had always been native to whatever country they were living in at the time.

"And what agency is your father with, dear?" Lady Bennett probed.

Rachel was prepared for the question. "He's not with an agency. It's a private consulting firm with government contracts. He's in Japan right now." Her cool tone effectively halted further questions, her manner indicating that the nature of her father's actual job was something one didn't discuss. Lady Bennett was quick to change the subject, convincing Rachel that the implication of her answer—that her father was some sort of intelligence officer—had been accepted.

They stopped several times along the way so that it was dusk by the time they arrived at Jason Wilder's house. Linwood was located northeast of White River Junction, Vermont, south of New Hampshire's White Mountains. The countryside's rolling foothills were heavily treed with white pine, spruce, hemlock and white birch, with wildflowers often growing at the sides of the roads. As they left the highway and traveled along ever-narrower local roads Rachel began to understand just how much Jason Wilder must value his privacy. If he had been annoyed about the delivery of a car and horses, his reaction to the delivery of a cook was sure to be explosive. Lady Bennett was much too sly to have warned him in advance; Rachel was certain that her appearance would present yet another surprise, a fait accompli he would have to accept.

Eventually they drove through a set of heavy metal gates onto a graveled driveway. The gates were unlocked, presumably in expectation of Lady Bennett's arrival, but by now Rachel half-expected to see an armed guard with two Dobermans to keep out unwanted visitors.

The long driveway eventually curved up to meet a short stone path, which in turn led to Jason Wilder's two-and-a-half-story frame house, the wood grooved to resemble masonry. A separate garage stood some distance away. These buildings and the surrounding lawn comprised a half-acre oasis in the woods, the graceful Georgian classicism anachronistic in this primitive setting.

It was still light enough to see the details of the formal entryway, its double doors framed by carved columns of dark wood, a broken scroll pediment on top. There were two sliding sash windows on either side of the doors, with another two pairs directly above on the second floor, an elegant Palladian window between them. A row of attic dormers with triangular pediments protruded from the steeply pitched roof that angled toward the horizontal some two-thirds of the way up, allowing more usable space in the attic.

Rachel had studied architecture and design in college; in fact, the courses had been among her favorites. She remembered that this style dated to the mid- to late-eighteenth century. Since Lady Bennett had remarked that her son had moved the house from Portsmouth on the New Hampshire coast, it was clearly authentic, rather than a copy. If she liked nothing else about Jason Wilder, she had to admit that she shared his taste in architecture.

Lady Bennett hopped out of the van and trotted down the path, climbing up a triple step to the front door. She was about to knock when it opened.

Rachel watched through the window of the van as mother and son embraced. She noticed that Jason

Wilder looked shorter in person than on the screen and that his hair was longer than in his movie star days. He was wearing blue jeans and a wool plaid shirt and did not appear to have aged, at least from a distance. At his side was a beautiful Irish setter that Lady Bennett reached down to pet. Its tail wagged in vigorous welcome, terminating Rachel's fantasies about vicious guard dogs. The setter would probably lick the hand that stole the silver.

As mother and son approached, Rachel was stunned to feel a wave of raw hostility wash over her. All the anger and hurt surfaced and she knew that if she didn't mask her feelings Jason Wilder was going to sense her antagonism—and wonder at the reason for it.

They were half-way to the van, walking arm in arm, when Rachel climbed out, her wrinkled coat draped over her shoulders to ward off the slight New England chill. Jason gave her body an insultingly thorough inspection and then drawled to his mother, "Is she another one of your presents? To go with the horses and the freezer and the mattress? Because if she is, I think I prefer the newest mare."

"Don't be beastly, darling," Lady Bennett scolded. "She's the cook. Her name is Miss Grant and she's an absolute treasure. I won't have you tossing out clever insults simply because you're peeved with *me*. Now apologize."

To Rachel's surprise, Jason Wilder did so, although in the least convincing of tones. Now that he was directly in front of her Rachel could see the age lines about his eyes and mouth, the earlier boyishness muted by strength and a trace of cynicism. Her initial impression of his height had been correct. In the tennis shoes he was wearing he was probably about five feet, ten inches tall. No doubt he had worn boots with two or three inch heels when stomping around the galaxy as Hamlin Stone, his costumes designed to reinforce the impression of tallness.

She stood leaning against the van, forcing herself to appear relaxed even though she felt stiff with tension. "How do you do, Mr. Wilder?" she asked politely.

"Very well, thank you, Miss Grant," he said, mimicking her schoolgirl tone so perfectly that she was tempted to smile in appreciation. He looked at his mother. "I don't care if she's cooked for the queen, Mother, she's going back to New York with Richards. Karen can take care of your friends."

"I wouldn't think of it. In the first place, Jason, the girl is a dreadful cook, and in the second place, she has quite enough to do with a family and three different jobs to look after." Lady Bennett gazed up into her son's blue eyes, her expression both plaintive and mischievous. "She'll make all your favorite dishes, Jason. The most divine little turnovers— Latin American. Jackie tasted onion soup that . . ."

"No, Mother." Jason Wilder removed his arm from his mother's waist and stepped to the side, his expression more long-suffering than angry. "I'm putting up with your friends and your horses, but there's a limit to what you can inflict on me, and having Miss Grant in my home surpasses it."

Men were usually aroused by Rachel's company, not annoyed by it. She realized that a feminine urge to be appreciated had joined her hostile attitude to this man. "I'm getting cold, Mr. Wilder," she pointed out, careful to keep her tone respectful. "Perhaps we could discuss this . . ."

"It might help if you didn't walk around half-naked," he interrupted irritably, adding some muttered reference to the younger generation and its lack of common sense. He glanced over at Richards, who had opened the back doors of the van, removed the luggage and was carefully sliding the crate of meat along the floor. "What on earth is in there?" he asked.

"The meat, darling," Lady Bennett reminded him.

"Of course," he muttered, his eyes looking skyward in exasperation. "The meat. How could I have forgotten the meat?" He walked over to help Richards unload the crate, telling his mother, "I hope you realize that I'm not going to risk my back and my floors by dragging this thing inside."

Lady Bennett followed him with her eyes, the calculating gleam in them telling Rachel that she was debating just how far she could push him. Apparently she decided that he had indeed reached the limit of his tolerance because after a few moments she clucked soothingly, "Naturally, darling. You can leave it on the walk. It will stay colder outside, anyway, and Miss Grant and I will unpack it in the morning."

Jason shot her a quelling look at the reference to "Miss Grant," but said nothing as Rachel and Lady Bennett preceded the men inside. The entrance was an absolute delight. The front hall, containing similar inlaid chests on opposite walls, each one flanked by a pair of upholstered chairs, was a charming little waiting room. It widened into a spacious salon furnished with period antiques, the opening between the two areas framed by a graceful wooden arch. The stairway angled toward the front of the house, with the second-story landing almost directly above the front door. Delicate spiral-turned balusters supported the handrail. Both rooms were paneled in dark wood, with fluted pilaster accents, and the plank floors were covered with oriental rugs.

"I want you to appreciate what I've done for your bloody freezer, Mother," Jason said, his tone relatively equable despite his choice of adjectives. Everyone obediently trailed after him, passing through a door off the salon into the kitchen. Although small, the room was completely modern, with new appliances, blue and white tiled counters and a no-wax floor. They continued into a utility room, dodging stacked-up cartons which rested in the center of the floor.

"You see these cartons? They contain food, Mother. And the reason they contain food is that we had to rip out an entire wall of shelves"—he pointed to his left—"in order to accommodate your freezer. My house, you might have recalled, is rather small and, in fact, could fit into one corner of that blasted Tudor mansion you live in." Having made his point, he stalked out of the room, the other three following like chastened baby ducks. Rachel couldn't help smiling. Considering the inconvenience his mother had caused him, it was a wonder he wasn't far more uncivil than he was. Her intense hostility of only fifteen minutes before began to fade a little.

The two men returned to the van, taking several trips to bring in Lady Bennett's luggage. "Only seven cases?" Jason asked, staring at the bags, which were now lined up in a neat row at the foot of the steps. "Traveling light these days, aren't you?"

Lady Bennett ignored his gibe, just as she had ignored all his other signs of ill-temper. "And now Rachel's things, darling," she said.

"I said no, Mother." Jason was, Rachel noticed, beginning to exhibit some genuine anger, as opposed to his earlier irritation.

"Of course you did, Jason. But she'll need her toothbrush and nightie, won't she?"

"Then let her carry them in herself!" he snapped. He sighed, his features softening a little as he kissed his mother good-night. "I'm going back to work," he told her. The last Rachel saw of him was his back, heading up the staircase, the dog trotting along behind him.

"Oh, dear!" In spite of the exclamation, Lady Bennett was not in the least bit distressed. Richards winked at her and started out the front door and Rachel hurried after him. When they came back in with her suitcases, Lady Bennett opined that her son was best left to his own devices for the moment, then favored Richards with one of her most saintly smiles. "Why don't you spend the night in Lebanon, Richards? You can get an early start in the morning." A white envelope with an embossed return address was gingerly withdrawn from her purse and slipped into his waiting hand, along with her warmest thanks. He executed a slight bow and left the house.

Lady Bennett's strategy was immediately apparent. With Richards back in New York, Rachel would be forced to stay at the house, at least until transportation could be arranged. "Lady Bennett—Olivia—" she began in protest.

"Of course! I've forgotten to show you where your room is, haven't I?" She took Rachel's arm. "I'm going to tackle Jason after a little while, dear, but do come back down and look through the rest of the house once you're settled in."

Rachel, uncharacteristically indecisive, stared at her luggage and then picked up only the overnight case. Recalling Jason's anger, she felt she should have listened to Susan's warning. But how could she have known that Jason Wilder's temper would already be provoked by meat, a freezer, a car, horses and a mattress?

Lady Bennett led her up the stairs into a charming bedroom decorated in blue and white with eighteenth-century style fabrics and period furniture that Rachel spotted as good-quality reproductions. "My bedroom is next door. We share a bath," Lady Bennett told her. "There's a master suite on the other side, but Jason won't use it. He's turned the attic into his own private lair. You really must have a peek up there. It was quite a project restoring the house, moving the walls about and so forth. Not to mention bringing it all the way from the coast. But Jason can be very determined when he wants something." She smiled at Rachel. "It's a quality he inherited from his mother."

"I think he'll send me packing in the morning, Olivia," Rachel said. "What he wants *now* is to see the back of me."

"You leave Jason to me. He doesn't realize that he has to rejoin the world, dear, but I've resolved that he's hidden himself away for quite long enough. I'll grant you that at the moment, he's out of sorts about the meat and the freezer and the horses, although I can't think why."

Her gurgle of laughter belied her protestation of puzzlement. "I'm off to beard the lion in his den," she said. "Fortunately, he adores good food and his little housekeeper—Karen—can't do a thing beyond a dreadfully runny stew. It's an argument in our favor." She bid Rachel good-night and headed toward the stairs.

At least, Rachel thought with relief, Jason Wilder had given no sign of recognizing her—although, considering the fact that his mother was in the process of turning his whole life inside out, it was hardly surprising that he had scarcely noticed Rachel, regarding her as just one more thorn in his paw. She wondered who would win the coming skirmish. Lady Bennett had a unique way of coping with opposition. She simply pretended that all objections were trivial, and thus beneath discussion, and then proceeded to do exactly as she pleased. Unfortunately for her, her son had had thirty-seven years in which to develop an effective counterattack. Although Rachel now understood that Lady Bennett's motive for this invasion was maternal concern, she ~ ˡ a twinge of sympathy for the unwilling rescuée.

As Lady Bennett had suggested, Rachel returned downstairs to look through the rest of the house. The large front parlor, like the entrance salon, was paneled in dark wood, with shell-topped cupboards inset on either side of a brick fireplace. A bronze and glass chandelier was suspended from the stuccoed ceiling, the furniture a mixture of antiques in the Queen Anne and Chippendale styles of the eighteenth century. The library beyond, with its round table and chairs, perhaps meant for card playing, and its upholstered easy chairs for reading, was of the same period. Both were connected to a modern powder room.

The dining room, on the other side of the staircase, was more eclectic than the rest of the first floor.

Chinoiserie wallpaper in relatively muted shades depicted a Chinese village nestled into the hills of the countryside. The fireplace was framed in gray-veined white marble, and lacked the elaborate wood mantel of the one in the parlor. The furniture, including an oval dining table with eight chairs around it, was from a later period and featured straight, classical lines.

Nothing in this house was short of enchanting, Rachel thought, with the exception of its owner. How could he have such flawless taste in design—and such appalling taste in subject matter for his novels? How could he nurture his privacy so zealously—and violate her own so totally? And most puzzling of all, how could the forbearing, if irritated, son she had met tonight be the same man as the cruel, obsessive husband of *Tinseltown?*

# Chapter Three

$\mathcal{R}$achel woke up just after six-thirty and lay in bed for several minutes, listening to the unaccustomed music of birds defending their territories. After four years in New York City she could now sleep through crashing garbage cans, delivery trucks and sirens, but the singing of birds had apparently awakened her.

A cookbook, still open to a section of veal recipes, rested on the nighttable. It was the only item Rachel had carried upstairs the night before. Given Jason Wilder's hostility to her presence in this house, it had seemed politic to leave her luggage in the downstairs hall, an announcement that she had yet to settle in.

Her overnight bag contained only her toiletries and sleepwear; if she wanted to get dressed, she would have to pull out a change of clothing from her larger suitcase. After a stop in the bathroom, she opened the bedroom door, almost expecting to find her luggage sitting outside in the hall, carried upstairs by a recalcitrant but defeated master of the house. The expectation proved overly-optimistic. Lady Bennett had obviously lost the first round.

Rachel walked back to the closet to fetch her robe. A glance into the mirror on the back of the door revealed tangled hair and sleepy eyes that made her look closer to twenty than thirty. Pulling on the ankle-length terrycloth bathrobe over her flannel nightgown, she started downstairs, the wooden steps cold against her bare feet.

Lady Bennett's luggage was gone now, but Rachel's two bags sat exactly where she had left them the night before, tucked under the rising staircase in the downstairs hall. Rather than sitting on the floor and rummaging around for the outfit she wanted, she picked up the suitcase with her clothing in it and started back upstairs. She had just reached the top when a low drawl interrupted her.

"Hunkering down for the duration, Miss Grant?" Jason Wilder asked her.

Rachel set the suitcase down and looked to her right. Jason was wearing a calf-length bathrobe of a burnished brown color, styled similarly to her own. Unlike herself, however, he obviously wore nothing underneath. "My jeans are in here," she said.

"Leave it for now. I want to talk to you."

"As soon as I dress . . ."

"I said now." Although his soft, firm tone was one that most people would instinctively obey, Rachel was not "most people." She arched an eyebrow in ironic inquiry, questioning him even though both of them knew exactly what he wanted to talk to her about.

When he ignored her silent query and started back toward the attic steps, she said to his retreating figure, "Is a bathroom break permitted, Mr. Wilder?"

He stopped. Rachel suspected that he realized that she had no need for the facilities—that her question was a subtle assertion of independence, a way of forcing him to wait until she was ready to deal with him. But he could hardly refuse the request. "I'll be upstairs," he said after a brief pause and then continued down the hall.

Rachel took a minute to brush out her hair, considered dressing and decided against it. She was not about to announce to the man that sitting in front of him in a bathrobe made her at all uncomfortable. After all, she was a twenty-eight-year-old widow, not a teenage virgin.

The hall widened into a small second-story parlor with the staircase to Jason Wilder's attic domain directly above the staircase from the first floor. Rachel reached the top to find herself looking into an office. The floor plan up here was an open one, with all walls except the structurally necessary ones removed. The office was furnished with utilitarian, though attractive, oak furniture; stacks of books, magazines and newspapers covered every available surface. Jason Wilder might prefer antiques in his home, but there was nothing old-fashioned about his office. He owned both a portable photocopier and a word-processor. A half-finished manuscript page was rolled through the carriage of the latter.

On the other side of the fireplace wall was a sitting room, also furnished with contemporary pieces, including a portable television set. Rachel glanced down the corridor that led to the rooms on the other side of the staircase. Strung out along its length were a pool table, two video games—an interstellar combat model and baseball—and a table-model hockey game. Either Jason Wilder routinely pressed the housekeeper into service as an opponent or he was not quite the recluse his mother supposed him to be.

Obviously, Rachel thought to herself, the man enjoyed playing games. At the moment, the game they seemed to be playing was "Hide and Go Seek." She walked past the penny arcade to his bedroom. Since there was no door, she found herself looking straight at Jason Wilder, who was lying on the king-sized bed, his hands clasped behind his head, eyes closed. His robe had fallen open, providing an enticing glimpse of his powerful chest.

He knows I'm standing here, Rachel told herself. Point two to him. "If I was 'it', you've just been found. Is it *my* turn to hide now?" she asked aloud.

She saw his lips twitch just slightly before he opened his eyes and cocked an eyebrow at her, imitating her earlier ironic gesture. She'd already known that the man had a sense of humor and his reaction was further evidence of it. Rachel, too tempted to resist, took her eyes from Jason's face, very deliberately swung them to the bathroom door, and then looked back at Jason. The man was so handsome that she had to remind herself about the book he had written and about her reason for coming up here.

He had no discernible reaction to her display of oneupmanship. "How much will it cost me to get you to clear out of here, Miss Grant?" he asked.

Rachel was prepared for a summary dismissal, not a drawled attempt at bribery which she suspected was only half-serious. She might have asked him how much he was offering but for the fact that she wanted to stay on the offensive in this conversation. So she affected puzzlement and asked him, "Why are you so anxious to get rid of me?"

"How much?" he repeated, now smiling at her with genuine amusement.

"I don't want your money." Rachel offered no explanation beyond this cool rejoinder—that would have been poor strategy, indeed.

He stretched, then swung off the bed and adjusted the belt of his bathrobe, making it snugger. "What's your first name?"

The question made Rachel nervous, but she answered it in the same cool tone she had used before.

"Rachel," he repeated. "Why don't we continue this conversation in the den? It's going to take longer than I thought it would."

As he walked toward her, Rachel noticed the graceful way he moved, a legacy of his training as a classical actor. She stepped back to let him pass, wanting to avoid physical contact, confused by her conflicting emotions. A surge of anger pierced her and yet, at the same time, she felt intensely attracted to him. He's seen deeper into my soul than any man in the world, she thought as she followed him, and yet he has no inkling of it. What a bizarre situation I've gotten myself into.

In the den, she waited until he sat down on the couch, then took the loveseat opposite, tucking her chilled feet up under her robe. A partially-opened carton stamped with a publisher's logo sat on the table between them and Rachel unthinkingly leaned forward to glance inside. What she saw destroyed her composure. It contained copies of the paperback edition of *A Latin American Tragedy*. She remembered the hell that book had put her through and felt herself pale.

"Is something the matter?"

Rachel hadn't realized that her eyes were fixed on the dramatically bloody covers until Jason's words brought her out of her trance. "It's very graphic—the cover of your book," she murmured, hoping he would assume she had a weak stomach when it came to artwork.

"Lurid would be a better adjective. But the publisher claims it sells books." He paused a moment to study her, watching her compose herself. "Have you read it?" he asked.

Rachel nodded. "It was very convincing." And who, she thought a little hysterically, should know better than I?

There was a brief silence. Rachel wondered what thoughts were hidden behind Jason Wilder's poker-faced expression. "So tell me about yourself," he said. "What's it like being the daughter of a spy?"

From the moment she had come upstairs Rachel had sensed that Jason was attracted to her, that he had mixed feelings about sending her away. If the teasing overtones of his last question were any guide, the feelings were no longer mixed. She could unpack her bags and settle in till Labor Day.

Even though it was obvious that he doubted the tall tale she had spun for Lady Bennett, Rachel decided to play it straight with her answer. "My father is an economist for a private consulting firm," she told him. "I'm a caterer and baker. There's nothing more to tell."

"Sure there is. Why would a beautiful woman want to hide herself away in a corner of New England cooking for successive waves of middle-aged people? Hiding out from foreign agents?" He grinned and winked at her. "Or did you come up here to compare my much-vaunted screen technique with the real thing?"

Actors learned to be charming, Rachel reminded herself, refusing to succumb. It was as phony as it was automatic, right down to the expertly delivered self-mockery of that last question. "Thank you for the compliment about my looks, Mr. Wilder. I came to New England in search of good weather, good riding and good company. It never occurred to me," she added sweetly, "that the last of those three delights would include the use of your body."

His smile grew into a gust of laughter. "I think you've overcome my objections to your presence, Rachel. You're older than I thought you were when we met last night, and sexy even at seven in the morning. Best of all, you're quick with a good line. I would be delighted to let you use my body." He patted a spot on the couch next to his thigh. "Come sit with me and try it out."

In spite of his smile, the invitation was a serious one. Did he really think she was the type of woman who let a man make love to her after only a few minutes in his company? Rachel asked herself. Or was he so accustomed to female admiration that a refusal was beyond his experience?

"No, thank you, Mr. Wilder." She rose from the loveseat. "If we've settled the problem of my employment, I'll leave you to the local talent."

"The local talent bores me. Now you, on the other hand . . ." In lieu of finishing the sentence, he stood up, then murmured, "Would you like me to seduce you, Rachel?"

"No, Mr. Wilder." Rachel felt herself blush with

embarrassment, something she hadn't done in years. In spite of her lingering animosity toward Jason Wilder, he probably *could* have seduced her. She remembered her fantasies about him and realized that she had better put some verbal distance between them. "What I'd like is for you to stop trying to bribe me, stop cross-examining me and stop propositioning me. What I'd like is for you to leave me alone."

"That's *my* line," he laughed. "Reclusive author and all that." He glanced at his watch. "When we met in the hall I was on my way to the kitchen to make myself breakfast and a pot of coffee to take upstairs. Since you're awake, you can take care of the coffee and fix me the breakfast."

Rachel readily agreed, quite willing to discuss her duties with him. After all, it *was* his house. Although she had been hired by Lady Bennett to cook for her and her guests, she told him, she was also happy to prepare his meals anytime he asked her to.

Jason shook his head. "As you might have noticed, I try to indulge my mother's whims. At times she leaves me little choice. But I told her last night that I'm not going to have someone working and living in my house who isn't subject to my authority. *I'm* paying your salary, Rachel."

He paused, perhaps to judge her reaction. At first bridling at the notion of taking orders from Jason Wilder, Rachel quickly decided that it didn't matter to her *who* made out her paychecks. Her face remained devoid of expression.

"Looking at you now makes me wish I'd been born in the Middle Ages," he went on, his gaze lazily seductive. *"Droit du seigneur* had a lot to commend it."

"Save that line for one of your novels," Rachel shot back. "In the 1980s it constitutes sexual harassment."

"I think I've been put in my place." He was laughing, not at all put out by her dart. "I apologize. As for *your* place—right now, it's in the kitchen, ma'am."

Rachel was positive that he was dying to add some crack to the effect that, later on, he would prefer her place to be in his bedroom. To his credit, he managed to restrain himself. Considering how charmingly he took rejection, Rachel couldn't be seriously annoyed by his propositions. He seemed to enjoy her flip way of saying "no" almost as much as he would have enjoyed a "yes," and though the sexual chemistry between them was undeniable she wasn't worried about a heavy physical pass. In her experience, a confident, mature man made sure that the lady was enthusiastic before making his first move.

The problem was not to appear enthusiastic when some all-too-human part of her wanted the same thing he did. In her three and one-half years as a caterer Rachel had fended off everyone from elderly butchers to eligible New York bachelors with a penchant for leering at her as she worked in their kitchens. The flannel nightgown and terry-cloth robe she wore right now were hardly sensual, especially compared to the clothing she and Susan sometimes wore on the job, yet Jason had only to glance at her to make her acutely aware of her body. He disturbed her, and seriously so.

It was such an unfamiliar sensation after all these years that Rachel had difficulty coping with it. Faced with the reality of a man who exuded sex appeal and charm, she found her feelings even more confused than before. She was certain of only one thing: becoming involved with Jason Wilder would be a horrible mistake.

She started down the steps, Jason calling after her that he would join her in a minute, and adding his order for breakfast. "Hash browns, ham and two scrambled eggs, and make the coffee strong."

As she poked around in the refrigerator, looking for the ingredients she would need, Rachel wondered if he ate this much every morning and, if so, whether he fixed it himself. Certainly the housekeeper didn't. By all reports, she was a disaster in the kitchen.

Jason reappeared just as Rachel located a frying pan. He held out two thick white socks of the type worn for sports. "I noticed your feet were cold. Are your slippers in the suitcase?"

"I don't own any. Thanks." She took the offering, smiling because he hadn't drawled out some obvious comment to the effect that he'd be happy to warm her feet for her any time she wanted him to.

He caught her look, seemed to know the reason for it, and grinned back. "I'm trying to be good," he protested. "Nobody ever accused me of sexual harassment before."

"Only the other way 'round, hmm?" Rachel shot back.

He laughed and sat down on a stool, taking a magazine from the counter and flipping through the pages. From time to time he glanced up, watching Rachel work. There was nothing offensive about those brief looks—he was attracted to her and saw no reason to hide it—but Rachel felt like her composure was under attack. The fact that he wasn't deliberately trying to unnerve her made his scrutiny even more disturbing, so that by the time she placed his meal on the counter it was all she could do to reply to his pleasant, "Thanks, Rachel," with an equally pleasant, "You're welcome, Mr. Wilder." She struggled to achieve a measured retreat from the kitchen.

Back upstairs, Rachel closed her door and dropped wearily onto the bed, her head propped up against the pillows. Even Carlos hadn't had this effect on her and she had been so much younger then, so much less able to control her emotions. Of course, she wouldn't have admitted that at the time. She had considered herself, at twenty-one, the epitome of feminine beauty and sophistication.

She had met Carlos Garcia Martinez at a dinner party given in honor of his father by the French ambassador. Rachel was accustomed to attending those kinds of affairs; her mother's health had been delicate at the time and her father had often asked her to partner him. Thomas Grant was a career diplomat who had worked his way up to an ambassadorship in Santandia and Rachel, after having lived all over the world, had acquired quite a polished veneer.

She had learned to take the attentions of wealthy businessmen like Carlos Garcia Martinez in stride. He was in his late thirties and Rachel found him to be very handsome, very smooth. Any woman would have been flattered to be singled out by such a charming man, but she knew that Latins enjoyed giving extravagant compliments and did not take him seriously.

They met again two months later, at a pool party given by a mutual acquaintance. This time Carlos followed up his show of interest with an invitation to dinner. Although he was far older than the boys Rachel usually dated, she didn't feel uncomfortable with him. She was used to socializing with people of her parents' generation.

They became engaged that Christmas. Rachel's parents were not enthusiastic about having their daughter marry a man eighteen years her senior, especially given their differing cultural backgrounds. She knew that even though they gave the match their approval they hoped that she would break her engagement before the wedding in June.

There was never a question of her doing so. She thought she was in love with Carlos Garcia Martinez. Certainly she loved the elegant parties he escorted her to, the deference with which people greeted her and her fiancé's smooth charm and impeccable manners. When she pictured herself as mistress over his beautiful home and numerous servants a warm flush of pleasure suffused her whole body. She had no doubts about the physical side of marriage. Although Carlos's lovemaking during their engagement never progressed beyond gentle kisses, Rachel enjoyed it when he touched her and looked forward to sleeping with him. He was a thirty-nine-year-old Latin American, she told herself, not an American boy in his twenties, and his restraint reflected both his respect for her and the customs of his society.

Looking back on it later, Rachel understood that she had married for the most superficial of reasons and that her outward sophistication had masked a shallow naïveté and embarrassing vanity. It had seemed so perfect at twenty-two: to run Carlos's home, bear his children and take her proper place in Santandian society.

Their wedding night provided her first disappointment. Having grown up with explicit novels and romantic movies she expected torrid passion mingled with tender regard. Carlos was considerate and gentle, but he gave little thought to her pleasure. She gradually realized that he considered sexual gratification the province of men. As his wife, she was placed firmly on a pedestal, expected to submit but not to enjoy. He seemed to take the attitude that since his demands were not excessive she had no cause for complaint.

When Rachel tried to discuss her feelings of disappointment with him he reacted by patronizing her. Like all American women, she made too much of sex, he said. Besides, she was young and inexperienced—once she had a child she would respond more fully.

Eventually Rachel found the courage to buy a well-known book on the subject of lovemaking, only to have Carlos throw it across the room, enraged. A real woman, he stormed, would have no such problems. She would understand a man's needs. It was not his fault if she was a frigid child.

A little frightened by his outburst, Rachel quickly dropped the subject. The next day Carlos apologized, saying that she was a lady, not a whore, and that she pleased him just as she was. Her restraint and coolness were desirable qualities in a young woman, something he had searched for. He completely ignored her lack of pleasure in their lovemaking, but Rachel had decided it was useless to argue. In any event, she considered the physical side of marriage to be of secondary importance.

She was busy giving dinner parties, playing Lady

Bountiful for local charities, visiting friends and shopping for clothes. Having lived in Latin America for several years she accepted these pursuits as both proper and enjoyable for a woman in her circumstances. After all, everyone who mattered praised her charm and flair.

Another six months passed, relatively uneventful ones. But then a new source of tension began to creep into her relationship with Carlos.

They had been married eight months and Rachel was not yet pregnant. At Carlos's insistence she consulted a prominent specialist in fertility problems who administered a raft of tests, often painful, but could find nothing wrong with her. He diagnosed the problem as too much activity and tension and prescribed rest and tranquilizers. Rachel tried to slow down but found inactivity boring; as for the pills, she washed a few down the drain every day so Carlos would think she was taking them.

After a few more months went by without a pregnancy Rachel hesitantly suggested to Carlos that *he* might visit a doctor. At first he refused, treating her request as a joke, but when she pressed the issue he informed her in the most condescending of tones that he had fathered a son by his mistress, with another child on the way. Surely she had known that there could be nothing wrong with *his* potency.

In fact, Rachel hadn't known. She was shocked to learn that Carlos had ever had a mistress, and appalled that the relationship had continued after their marriage. When she confided her feelings to her closest friend the woman merely shrugged. Many wealthy men maintained a *casa chica*, including her own husband, the woman told Rachel. It had nothing to do with Carlos's love and respect for Rachel, but was simply the Santandian way. She would have to accept it.

Rachel might have done so, but by now she was beginning to realize that her marriage to Carlos had been a mistake—one of many mistakes she had made in her life. She felt as if she had aged years in her twelve months as his wife, but even had her relationship with Carlos been a good one boredom with her daily routine and disappointment in her own superficiality would still have set in.

Socializing, entertaining and endless shopping had ceased to be enjoyable, much less meaningful to her. She regretted leaving school after three years of doing only the minimum amount of work and made tentative, ineffectual efforts at self-education. When she looked in the mirror she saw a woman who was suited for nothing beyond her current role as a wealthy man's ornament. Since she hadn't produced a child, Carlos valued her very little. True, he was pleased by her social success and proud of the way other men admired her red-haired beauty, but Rachel, once so vain about her looks, had come to realize that they would fade in time and that knowing how to arrange flowers was precious little in the way of a replacement. She had never bothered to develop herself as an individual.

Her parents had gone back to Washington where Thomas Grant was on temporary assignment at the State Department. Rachel knew she was drifting, but she had no one to turn to for advice or help and no inner resouces to fall back on. By the time eight more months had passed her marriage was no more than a social convention. She and Carlos acted the devoted couple in public and ignored one another in private.

Forced to cope with the situation on her own, Rachel began to toy with the idea of getting an annulment based on her failure to bear children. On the spring day that Carlos was kidnapped she had finally promised herself that she would phone a local attorney for an appointment.

The next week was a hellish one. The police soon announced that her husband and a business associate had been captured by terrorists, but there was no ransom demand. Attempts to locate the two men were unsuccessful. The house was constantly under siege by newsmen and Rachel, who spoke fluent Spanish, became adept at looking straight into their cameras and telling them in a husky voice that she had had no news of her husband.

It wasn't entirely a performance. She still had some feeling for Carlos and earnestly hoped for his safety. She blamed herself as well as him for the failed marriage, feeling guilty about her barrenness and wondering if her own sexual ineptitude had caused him to maintain his relationship with his mistress. But she was not as distraught as a loved and loving wife would have been and knew she was a hypocrite for pretending to be.

As the weeks passed the media types drifted away, and the story receded from page one to page ten and then out of the papers entirely. Three months after the kidnapping, the partially decomposed body of Carlos's associate was found in the jungle, identified through dental records. Rachel's family had been urging her to leave Santandia and she finally took their advice. She moved in with her sister Susan in

New York, resumed her maiden name and registered for the fall semester at college as an English major.

Unlike Rachel, Susan had stopped living with their parents when she was fourteen and had attended prep school in New England and then college and cooking classes in both Paris and New York. In addition to running her newly-established business, Grant Catering, she taught several cooking classes for nonprofessionals. One was for men only, and it was there that she met Dr. Philip Lenglen. The two became engaged in January, shortly after Rachel decided to add her talents to Susan's business.

Although Rachel lacked her sister's formal training, she had always enjoyed cooking, and had learned dozens of foreign specialties by watching and helping the Grants' various cooks. A typical reformed sinner, she took her college work seriously, but the energy she put into Grant Catering was even greater than the energy she devoted to her studies. Her efforts in both areas paid off with success, rewarding her with a sense of accomplishment that encouraged her to work even harder.

Her second career, as a freelance writer, was the result of a lucky break. She and Susan had catered a buffet luncheon for a prominent literary hostess and one of the guests, a magazine editor, had mentioned that her publication would welcome an article on the catering business. By then Rachel was studying for a master's degree in journalism. She was the logical one to take on the challenge and the results were excellent. Over the next two years she sold eight articles, all of them in the areas of gourmet cooking and entertaining.

The death of Carlos Garcia Martinez was confirmed in January, six months after Rachel had left

Santandia. When she returned for the funeral she learned that the bulk of his estate had been divided equally between his late brother's two adult sons. She had no quarrel with the arrangement, which was perfectly legal under Santandian law; after all, Carlos had married her to bear his children and, since she had failed to do so, it was only logical that his closest blood relations should inherit his money.

Her sister married Philip Lenglen the following June, leaving Rachel without an apartmentmate. By then, however, the business had become successful enough to allow her to manage financially on her own. She was too busy discovering herself to become lonely. School and work took up most of her time, with free hours devoted to museums, the theater, reading—all of the activities, in short, which she felt would remedy what she perceived as a repugnant shallowness and ignorance. Susan repeatedly told her that she was flailing herself unreasonably, but then, Susan didn't understand the life she had led in Santandia.

Until the discovery of her husband's body Rachel had considered herself to be married. Afterward, with a little prodding from Susan, she started to date again. She learned two things: first, that there was nothing wrong with her physically, and second, that she had no desire to let a man too close emotionally. She enjoyed going out, but always called a halt before any emotional involvement could develop. She felt that her reluctance to commit herself stemmed primarily from the fact that she was enjoying her independence too much to make the compromises a good relationship required. At the age of twenty-six she was no longer Ambassador Thomas Grant's daughter or Don Carlos Garcia Martinez's wife but plain Rachel Grant, wonderful cook and promising writer. Her self-confidence and self-respect were growing, the wounds from her marriage healing.

The only emotional obligation she accepted was that of being Susan Grant Lenglen's big sister and best friend. The two were becoming increasingly close, with Rachel telling Susan more about her life with Carlos than she had ever thought she would reveal. Still, much was withheld: the causes of the self-hatred she had once felt so strongly; the intimate details of their lovemaking. It was natural that, when problems arose in Susan's marriage, she, in turn, would confide in Rachel.

Given Philip's inability to love and his apparent insecurity, Rachel could only encourage Susan to be reassuring and giving, even after Philip demanded that she abandon her career. His subsequent retaliatory affair and refusal to agree to marital counseling were something else again. Susan felt it impossible to stay with him, but even after making this decision she had needed a great deal of understanding and support, and Rachel had provided it.

By the time *A Latin American Tragedy* was published Rachel was twenty-seven years old, with numerous accomplishments to her credit and what she thought was a healthy sense of self-worth. As it turned out, three years of feeling good about herself couldn't compensate for twenty-four years of the opposite.

The publicity surrounding the novel reopened the trauma of her marriage and Carlos's death, their names usually mentioned in reviews as the book's inspiration. Every time Rachel saw the name

"Raquel Garcia Martinez" in print she felt sick to her stomach.

It was mortifying to read about Carlos's arrogance and male chauvinism and to learn that his long-time mistress had not been his only extra-marital involvement. Given the accuracy of Wilder's portrayal of *her,* however, Rachel never doubted that what he wrote about Carlos, the "Antonio" of the novel, was equally true. When she read the bedroom scenes between Maria and Antonio she cringed with humiliation. The analogous scenes with his mistress, Eva, at least provided some enlightenment about their problems in this area, even if Rachel found her discovery wholly repulsive. Carlos's preferences in bed, she felt, went far beyond what most people would have considered normal.

Jason Wilder had somehow gotten into both their heads, and all of it was in the novel: Carlos's polite disdain, patronization and boredom; her own vanity, shallowness and hypocrisy. The title of the novel was of course ironic. To the world, Rachel had pretended to be a brave young woman, gamely fighting back tears in the face of tragedy. The real tragedy, the book argued, was these two people, and their sham of a relationship.

It was Maria who received the author's most stringent condemnation. Antonio was a product of his culture and class, as Wilder made clear. But Maria, an American, had had every advantage and option and the intelligence and talent to take advantage of them. She had made all the wrong decisions, consistently taken the easy path, and he seemed furious with her for it.

For Rachel, the book was nothing short of devastating. It upset her that Susan, who had always respected her, had read such a merciless dissection of her character. She felt guilty about every short-coming, every failure, and seemed to look for rea-sons to deny the progress she had made in the three years since leaving Santandia. Her depression deep-ened until it was all she could do to function.

Susan, trying to cope with her separation from Philip, was in no condition to handle Rachel's prob-lems as well as her own. In any event, she lacked the necessary professional training. Philip still called regularly, however, and oddly enough it had been Philip, the man who had refused counseling for himself, who had given Rachel the name of a sympathetic woman therapist, and Philip who had finally persuaded her to make an appointment.

After several months of working with Dr. Ellen Quinby, Rachel came to understand that part of her depression had been caused by anger turned inward —justifiable anger at the way her life had been laid bare to public scrutiny. And just as Susan had pointed out to her, she had a self-destructive tenden-cy to judge herself too harshly. But the real root of her problem was an inability to accept her earlier behavior and move on, a fear that the changes she had made would prove to be ephemeral. In addition, she was afraid that if people identified her as the "Maria" of the novel they would reject her. As a result, she was prone to be wary of strangers, to keep people at a distance.

Two months earlier, Dr. Quinby had assured Rachel that her feelings were normal, and that she had made so much progress that regular sessions were no longer necessary. All she needed was enough time to feel confident about herself and the patience to give herself that time. There was nothing neurotic about her conflicting feelings toward Jason Wilder, Dr. Quinby added. It was quite natural that she should be both angry and intrigued.

So why had she really come to New Hampshire? She had told herself that her anger demanded assuagement, but would revenge accomplish that? Was she actually here to confront her own personal demon, to gain his approval? Or did she want him to fulfill the fantasies that she had previously found so disturbing?

Rachel didn't have the answers. After only an hour in Jason Wilder's company, after less than a day in his house, she was confused and unsettled. She hated the sensation of losing control over her life.

# Chapter Four

*R*achel opened her eyes, slowly becoming aware of the way her body was trembling. It had been months since she last woke up shaking, and the fierce hostility she had earlier felt toward Jason Wilder briefly flared up again, easing as she regained control. You are responsible for your own life, she reminded herself. Write the article if you feel you need to, but don't blame Wilder for all your problems. He might have written about them, but he didn't cause them, and only you can solve them.

Calmer after this silent pep talk, Rachel carried her suitcase in from the hall, then showered and dressed, pulling on jeans, a long-sleeved blouse and a crewneck sweater. She was brushing her hair into a ponytail when a light knock on the door interrupted her.

Her heart began to pound heavily even while she told herself that undoubtedly someone other than

Jason Wilder was on the other side of the door. Two firm raps would be more in character for the man than the same number of hesitant taps.

"Yes?" she called out, walking out of the bathroom.

Lady Bennett gingerly pushed open the door. She was dressed in wheat jodhpurs and a white blouse, a black riding jacket looped over her right arm. "I've had the loveliest time," she said to Rachel. "The horse Nancy Foxworth sent over is a dear. I saw the dishes in the sink. Did Jason wake you?"

Rachel's sense of humor came to the fore. "Good morning, Olivia. Tomorrow I'd love to join you. We met in the hallway at 6:45." Her answer subtly mocked Lady Bennett's habit of speaking in non sequiturs.

"It *does* disarm people," Lady Bennett admitted with a smile. "But I've been talking this way for so long that I believe it's become second nature by now, Rachel. I tackled him last night, you know. He carried on about his privacy, but in the end he gave in. I really don't understand why people find Jason so difficult. *I* never have any trouble with him."

"Maybe you're the only one who has the perseverence to outargue him," Rachel said. "We had an interesting conversation this morning, Olivia. First he tried to pay me off to leave and then he questioned my motives for being here. In the end he graciously offered to seduce me, not without a certain charm, I admit." Rachel found herself smiling at the memory of their confrontation. Jason *had* looked rather repentant, holding his peace offering of sweat socks out to her.

"How generous of him," his mother answered dryly. "Jason always was partial to redheads. He was married to one once, but of course, you know that. Everyone does. It was a terrible mistake, Rachel. She was totally wrong for him. It's only fair to warn you that he's had no use for commitments ever since."

"I'm twenty-eight years old, Olivia. I can take care of myself."

"Naturally, dear. I wouldn't have asked you to come if it weren't for your rather remarkable sang-froid. Inherited from your father, I expect." Lady Bennett's hand flew to her cheek in pretended chagrin at her lapse. "But one doesn't talk of that, does one?" She beamed at Rachel, said she would see her downstairs for breakfast and departed.

Obviously, Rachel told herself, Lady Bennett put no more credence in her hints about her father's occupation than Jason did. She would have to stick to her story that he was an economist. A few minutes later she entered the dining room to find Lady Bennett sitting at the table drinking a cup of coffee and thumbing through the book review section of a national magazine.

. She sat down, asking "What did they review this week? Anything interesting?"

"The maternal urge overcame me," Lady Bennett answered. "It only came out in paperback two weeks ago. They paid a ridiculous amount for the rights, but it's already in the top five on all the lists, so I suppose they'll finally stop nagging him about publicity tours. He won't do them."

She was looking at the best seller list, checking the position of *A Latin American Tragedy*. Rachel made the proper polite comment. "You must be very proud of your son."

"I'm proud of all my children," Lady Bennett

said. "But I think I should be honest with you, Rachel. There's a method to my madness."

It took Rachel a moment to put this observation into its logical context. "You mean for the horses and the guests . . ."

"And the cook and the freezer," Lady Bennett finished. "It's quite true, Rachel. Normally I don't descend on Jason in quite so intrusive a fashion, but Stephen Chapin wants him for the lead in his new play and I agree that it's time he returned to the stage. His friends visit him here, of course, but he tends to shut out too much of the world. It was that business with Meredith, you see. So I thought I'd bring the world to *him*. And I've rather dragged you into the middle of it, haven't I?"

It was the second time that Lady Bennett had referred to Jason's first wife, Meredith Lloyd. Rachel suspected that she did nothing without a motive. Why would she so carefully imply that her son had been the injured party in the marriage if not to gain him Rachel's sympathy? In spite of her earlier warning, was she angling for a love affair between Jason and Rachel, hoping that it would get his mind off his book?

If handled carefully, Rachel decided, Lady Bennett would be an excellent source of information about her son. "I'll forgive you," she said with a smile, "since it's so beautiful up here. But why do I have the feeling that Stephen Chapin will be coming up here later this month?"

"You're obviously psychic. Stephen's wife Paula—that's Jackie's sister, of course—is Jason's theatrical agent, you see. Not that she's made much money off him lately. And Harry Pollock is going to produce Stephen's play. All of us have known each other for years. Stephen first worked with Jason ages ago, when Jason was acting off Broadway. He wrote *Power Play* with Jason in mind as the lead, but he's so bloody obstinate that he refuses even to read it."

"Why is he so set against acting again?"

"His first marriage . . ." Lady Bennett stopped, then shook her head. "I *do* tend to let my tongue run away with me at times, Rachel. Fix yourself some breakfast and we'll have a tour of Linwood."

As Rachel scrambled an egg and toasted a slice of bread she came to the conclusion that Lady Olivia Bennett said exactly as much as she intended to and not one word more. Thus far, she had told Rachel nothing that wasn't grist for the public gossip mill. Eventually, however, the Chapins would show up in New Hampshire, and when they did, Rachel intended to monitor their conversations with Jason Wilder. The content was sure to prove illuminating.

After breakfast the two women walked out to the rental car, Jason's Irish setter trotting up to the door just as they were getting in. He wagged his tail beseechingly until Lady Bennett succumbed and issued an invitation to hop onto the back seat.

"Another one of Jason's redheads," she told Rachel. "His name is Synge. Jason is very fond of *The Playboy of the Western World*. He once played Christy, but he never quite got the accent right."

"A horse named Caligula after a character in a play and a dog named Synge after a playwright," Rachel mused aloud. "Frankly, Olivia, the amateur psychiatrist in me says that you'll have a hard time getting your son to act again."

"Do you think so?" Lady Bennett asked. "There was an Abyssinian cat once, but Jason gave him away. He scratched the furniture, and Jason couldn't bear to declaw him. They're the original Egyptian cats, you know, at least some people think so. His name was Omar."

"As in Sharif, and there goes my theory," Rachel smiled.

"Not entirely. Jason is an excellent bridge player. I believe Mr. Sharif's talent for cards was the inspiration for the name."

Rachel told Lady Bennett that she and Susan occasionally played in duplicate tournaments, although neither of them was an expert. "Maybe your son will find me less objectionable if I tell him I play bridge," she added.

"But that's not all you have in common, is it, Rachel?"

Rachel, caught off guard by Lady Bennett's question, started visibly.

Lady Bennett continued, "I understand from Jackie Pollock that you're quite a successful writer."

"Not in the same league as your son. I write about food and entertaining. I've never tried fiction."

At that moment a white-tailed deer and her fawn bounded out of the trees and across the road. Rachel, uncomfortable with the topic of conversation, found their timing a godsend. She was able to ask Lady Bennett about local wildlife without appearing to have changed the subject.

Was it possible, she asked herself later, that Lady Bennett knew exactly who she was and why she had agreed to come up to New Hampshire? True, it seemed fanciful—even paranoid—to think so, because the woman had lived in England for the past twenty-five years and no member of Rachel's family had even set foot in that country during the same length of time. There could be no personal connection. The fact that her son had written about Rachel did not imply that she would know any more about Rachel's background than any random reader.

And yet, something inside Rachel insisted that her talent as a cook was not the primary reason for Lady Bennett's invitation. The woman might be amusing and charming, but she was a schemer. In the end, Rachel supposed, her employer's motives were unimportant. What mattered was the fact of her presence. What mattered was her future course of action.

Linwood was a picture-book New England town from the spire on its whitewashed church to the scattering of frame houses surrounding the village center, to the narrow strip of grassy common between its bifurcated main street.

Far from bustling with activity, two of the local businesses were actually vacant and locked up: a clothing store and a restaurant. Lady Bennett explained that they would re-open in the wintertime. Although the highest peaks of the White Mountains lay to the north the terrain here was still hilly enough to support several ski areas. The town was much busier in winter, when it catered to the annual influx of skiers.

"Dreadful curiosity seekers, some of them," she said as she and Rachel walked down one side of the common, Synge trotting alongside. "Jason is frightfully inconsistent. Every now and then he'll invite them in, especially if they've written ahead. But he's far more likely to tell Karen to send the dog after them."

"Synge would probably escort them to the door," Rachel said. "Karen is the housekeeper?"

"Yes. Sweet little thing—such a shame about her husband. I met them last summer."

"Olivia . . ." Rachel began with a smile.

"Yes, yes, I know. I *was* getting to it, dear. Karen's husband Paul is a cabinetmaker. He helped restore Jason's house. Early last winter he was in a dreadful accident—an explosion—but he's young and strong and he's doing very well. Karen's been supporting the family in the meantime, but there are two little ones and it's difficult. Jason helped out, naturally."

Naturally, Rachel thought. The forbearing son, wronged husband, occasionally benevolent literary lion and generous employer—it wasn't the picture she had expected to receive. Was it an accurate one?

They passed a bank and a service station before Lady Bennett crossed the street to a green-shuttered white building that Rachel would have taken for someone's home but for the plaque near the door indicating that it was the public library. The master of this two-story domain, a Mr. Enos Pepper, greeted Lady Bennett with a thin smile which Rachel suspected constituted the height of gushing effusiveness for the man.

After they had chatted for several minutes about local politics, the weather and the season's most popular books Mr. Pepper remarked to Lady Bennett, "Read your husband's last book, Livie. Never knew old ruins could be so interesting."

Rachel suppressed a smile. Mr. Pepper, with his bald head and cadaverous frame, looked something like a proud old ruin himself. Lady Bennett pulled back the zipper of the canvas tote she was carrying and pulled out three books, one hardcover and two paperbacks. Rachel didn't have to look at the covers to know what the titles were.

"I brought these over for you, Enos, since my son is hopelessly remiss about the niceties. The hardcover edition is for you, of course, and the others for the library." She flipped open the hardcover copy. "You see this? Jason calls you his 'good friend'. One of the chosen few, I should think."

The taciturn librarian's thin lips moved not a millimeter. "I mind my own business, Livie. Good fences . . ."

"Make good neighbors; yes, I know," Lady Bennett finished. "Jason would certainly agree with that. Now you take good care of Rachel when she comes in to browse, won't you, Enos?"

Mr. Pepper gave a deliberate nod and ambled over to the desk to check out picture books for several young children. Lady Bennett and Rachel continued their stroll up the other side of the common, passing a small office building, the post office, and a pharmacy before stopping into an old fashioned general store. Lady Bennett introduced Rachel to two more elderly New Englanders, a Mr. and Mrs. DeFalco, and then took a shopping cart and wheeled it down an aisle, in search of "a few items." By the time they reached the check-out she had accumulated four bagsful of groceries, including fresh produce so beautiful that Rachel was surprised to find it in a small local market.

While driving back to the house Lady Bennett provided a running commentary on each of the town's proprietors, how many years he had lived in Linwood, what he did in the summer if his business was open only in winter, details of his family life. It was obvious that she had a talent for drawing out these close-mouthed people because she told Rachel that in the five years that Jason had lived in New Hampshire she had visited him only seven times. Never before had she stayed for more than a few days, and yet she seemed to know all the local gossip.

"I suppose Jason knows I'm up to something," she said, "descending on him with all my paraphernalia this way, but he hasn't said so. Just gives me those long-suffering looks of his and goes about his business."

Lady Bennett pulled the car around to the back entrance off the kitchen and discovered the crate of meat sitting near the door. A hand truck was lying on the ground nearby. After unloading the groceries the women set to work unpacking the meat, which had been wrapped in freezer paper and labeled by cut and weight.

Afterward Lady Bennett excused herself to take a nap. Rachel, restless with the slower pace of life up here, occupied herself by baking bread: two loaves of white and one of rye. While it was rising she rearranged the food in the pantry and cleaned out the refrigerator, keeping a running inventory in her head as she worked. She concluded that the house was adequately stocked with both staples and specialty foods. If some of the more esoteric items called for in her recipes proved to be unavailable she could always try some creative substitutions.

Lady Bennett reappeared just after one-thirty. "That smells divine," she said, catching the aroma of the fresh-baked bread. "I can't possibly limit myself to cottage cheese and fruit as I'd planned, can I?"

She walked into the pantry, returning with a large

can of tuna fish. Rachel, watching her remove a jar of commercial mayonnaise from the refrigerator, wrinkled her nose in distaste and announced that it wasn't fit to eat. Although Lady Bennett protested that she would leave New Hampshire ten pounds heavier she didn't stop Rachel from plugging in the blender and taking out the eggs and oil.

As Rachel whipped the mayonnaise Lady Bennett cut herself a slice of white bread to go with the tuna salad. "He loathes tuna fish," she remarked cheerfully. "Hated it even as a child. Fix him a club sandwich, Rachel. That turkey in the refrigerator appears to have some life left in it. And another pot of black coffee. He's addicted to black coffee."

Rachel did as she was bidden, though not without misgivings. Jason Wilder had been quick enough to ask for breakfast this morning and if he had wanted lunch he would no doubt have come down and said so. But there was no point in arguing with Lady Bennett, as her son knew only too well.

As a professional cook Rachel disdained the idea of smearing bottled mayonnaise on a few slices of bread, slapping on some sort of filling and calling the result a decent sandwich. She was not averse to peanut butter and jelly for herself, but when she was preparing food for a customer nothing but the finest ingredients would do. Homemade bread and fresh mayonnaise were basics and, in addition, the lettuce had to be the crispest available, the tomato slices even and juicy, the bacon fried to perfection and the meat moist. The last requirement was a formidable one, given the condition of the turkey, but she managed to procure some suitable slices from a bird that was definitely past its prime. Her creation, cut into quarters and served with a dollop of fresh mayonnaise on the side, was as much a work of art as a club sandwich.

"Should I call him downstairs?" she asked Lady Bennett.

"Heavens, no!" From her tone, Lady Bennett clearly thought that Rachel had suggested something sacrilegious. "He's glued to that typewriter of his— quite uncivil if you catch him at the wrong moment. Just take it up to him and leave it on his desk—very quietly."

Rachel put the sandwich and the pot of coffee on a tray, only too aware of the way her sandals slapped against the hardwood stairs as she climbed to the attic floor. But Jason was typing, his back to the door, and didn't hear her approach over the sound of the machine.

She hesitated, waiting for him to stop, continuing forward with the tray only when he leaned back in his chair to think. He looked over his shoulder, removed a pair of gold-rimmed glasses and then frowned, first at her and then at the tray she held. She had the feeling that she had interrupted him in the middle of inventing some dazzling bit of dialogue and waited for the retaliatory fireworks.

His response, however, was comparatively mild. "Mother strikes again," he drawled. "Plug in the coffee pot and take the other one downstairs. You can feed the sandwich to the dog."

"My homemade bread and fresh mayonnaise . . ." Rachel bit off her instinctive protest, only to find Jason smiling at her contentiousness. She had to force herself not to stare at him. No man had a right to smile so attractively.

"Give me half, then." He placed the glasses on his desk. "I'm not much of a lunch eater, Rachel. Karen tries to foist off egg salad sandwiches on me, which I very politely thank her for and then turn over to Synge. Actually, he's something of a gourmet. I'm sure he'll enjoy your homemade bread a lot more than Karen's egg salad."

Attempting to ignore Jason's good-natured charm, Rachel set the tray on his desk, not bothering to clear away the books and notes underneath. The typing table was placed at a right angle to the desk, leaving Jason several feet away from her. He half-twisted his body to watch her as she reached over to unplug the empty coffee pot from a wall outlet and plug in the full one. A half-filled mug of cold coffee was sitting near the edge of the desk. Rachel left it there.

Although Jason made no move to touch her there was no mistaking the desire in his eyes. Rachel, angered again by the way he continued to implicitly raise the subject of sex, allowed her features to settle into a tight-lipped frown. It was a compromise between telling him off and pretending to be unaware of his all-too-obvious train of thought.

She removed half of the sandwich and set the plate on the desk, her motions brusque. "Don't look so disapproving," Jason told her softly. "The fact is, you interrupted a very hot scene. I was trying to describe how Rachid felt, in love with Yaël and taking her to bed for the first time. When you came into the room I began to envy him the release of his frustrations."

"I'll rinse this out for you." Rachel picked up the mug and stalked off to the bathroom. Her motive for this bit of housekeeping had nothing to do with a desire to be helpful and everything to do with the need to consider how to deal with Jason's provocative comments.

Tight-lipped disapproval didn't work. That left three options: she could ignore him entirely, discourage him with veiled sarcasm, or openly confront him. Over the past few years, she had found that the third method had the most lasting effect. Given her own mixed feelings, it might open her up to a potentially embarrassing discussion, but that was a risk she was willing to take. She would permit no man to continually proposition her, no matter how charming or subtle his technique.

Jason was eating the sandwich when she walked back into the office. "This is terrific," he told her. "You just changed my mind about lunches."

Rachel poured him a cup of coffee; it gave her something to do with her hands. "Would you mind bringing me half a sandwich and a fresh pot of coffee about one o'clock every day?" he asked.

"Not at all, as long as you don't transfer your hero's lusts to yourself and cast me in the role of your heroines," Rachel said. The irony in the sentence struck her the moment the words were out.

"I'm very attracted to you, Rachel. I want to make love to you and I see no point in pretending I don't. If I'm pushing it's because you're sending me a mixed message and I'm trying to find out what the hell is going on. You enjoy the verbal sparring, you look at me like you're attracted to me, but a few times now you've stiffened up like you can't stand my guts. Why?"

He was much too perceptive, sensing the conflict that Rachel had thought she'd kept hidden. Unwilling to give him an honest answer, she regarded him with a level, cool gaze and replied in her most peremptory manner, "I'm a grown woman, Mr. Wilder. If I want to sleep with you I'm capable of saying so. Until I do, the answer is no."

If Jason decided not to press her, Rachel sensed, it was only because he had come to the conclusion that it would be a waste of his time. After a short pause he said to her, "I think you need to know me better. I'm not what you think I am."

"And what would that be?"

"You think that *Tinseltown* is autobiographical. You think that I'm either a sadistic monster or a neurotic recluse, or maybe both."

"Are you always so dramatic?" Rachel mocked.

"Are *you* always so unresponsive?"

Rachel saw no point to their trying to score points off each other. Even if she was attracted to Jason Wilder she wasn't interested in a relationship with him. Of course, what he had suggested—a tumble on his bed—fell somewhat short of a relationship. She picked up the tray with its empty coffee pot and half-sandwich and silently walked away.

Back in the kitchen, Lady Bennett eyed the remainder of her offering with amusement, congratulating Rachel on persuading Jason to accept at least half of it. She was pleased to learn that her son had placed a daily order for lunch. In the end, Rachel finished the sandwich herself, donating a few scraps to Synge who, with canine ESP, had scratched at the back door just as she took her first bite.

The dog, as gentle as he was graceful, accompanied her on an afternoon inspection of the property. Rachel's first stop was Jason's garage. Parked alongside the jeep Lady Bennett had mentioned was a mid-sized American car, not an economy model, but hardly in the luxury class, either. Continuing on, Rachel located the barn Lady Bennett had spoken of at the bottom of a wooded hill, the horses grazing in the rolling pasture nearby. Caligula, a large chestnut Anglo-Arabian with two white stockings seemed placid enough as he nibbled at the grass, but Rachel wouldn't have ridden him on a dare. He looked up at her, insultingly uninterested, and then returned to his lunch.

One of the mares came up to the fence to invite Rachel to stroke her nose, prompting a quick apology. "I don't have anything to give you, love. Tomorrow I'll bring a lump of sugar; we'll go riding together." She stayed for several more minutes, talking to the mare and petting her neck.

There was a stand of white pine on the other side of the house, in the opposite direction from the barn. Rachel followed Synge as he trotted over the heavily needled ground, reaching down to reward him with a scratch on the head when he led her to a secluded glacial pond. It was fed by a mountain stream and, judging by its size, must have been dredged out for swimming and boating. A short wooden dock had been constructed on Rachel's side of the lake and a metal rowboat moored to one post.

Rachel hadn't rowed since her days as a teenage camper, but now she untied the boat and took it to the opposite shore. The bottom of the lake sloped more gradually here and she was able to drag the boat up onto the grass. Then she waded into the water. Although she found it far too cold for more than a fast dip, the lake was a perfect spot for sunbathing—private and serene. An overgrown dirt road led back through the trees on this side of the lake and Rachel followed it for a short distance before turning back. There were hoof marks but no tire tracks, indicating that the trail was used only for riding nowadays.

Sitting on the grass, her arms clasped around her legs, Rachel found herself thinking about Jason, wondering if he ever swam here. Presumably he was inured to the cold water by now. At the moment he was no doubt too absorbed in Yaël, Rachid and their mutual passion to tear himself away from his typewriter.

As for *her* passions—now there was a subject for her consideration. With Dr. Quinby's help she had learned to analyze and understand her feelings, but she couldn't remember having to make sense of so many conflicting ones at once. Even worse, they constantly shifted around, different feelings taking precedence at different times.

For the first time since her arrival, it struck Rachel that there might be an element of masochism in her decision to come to New Hampshire. On some level she supposed she wanted Jason Wilder to figure out who she was. But why? She had already acknowledged the wish to gain his approval, but was it possible that part of her might want his disapproval instead, as further punishment for the supposed sins of her past? It was a disturbing thought. She had believed that such destructive feelings were behind her.

She shook her head, rejecting the notion. The problem was that Jason wasn't at all what she'd anticipated. No matter how handsome he was, sarcasm, conceit and arrogance would have cancelled out any physical appeal. But there was little trace of the waspish cynic she had half-expected. On the contrary, his sense of humor and frequent displays of charm only reinforced every fantasy she had ever had about him.

She reminded herself that he was a very talented actor and that, therefore, it was impossible to know exactly how the "real" Jason Wilder normally behaved. Naturally, a man bent on seduction sought to entice the object of his desire. When his passions were assuaged, when he tired of her, he might quickly exhibit indifference or even dislike.

Rachel was too independent to predicate her actions on what Jason Wilder might or might not think about her. She accepted responsibility for her own life and her own happiness. At the moment she had some important decisions to make, the most pressing of which concerned the article she had planned to write. Although she was beginning to doubt that she would ever publish it, the compulsion to research it was even stronger than before. Jason was starting to intrigue her quite apart from her personal feelings toward him.

If *Tinseltown* wasn't autobiographical, why had he given people the impression that it was? To sell books? Out of some cynical need to demonstrate the gullibility of the public? Lady Bennett had indicated that his decision to give up acting had been connected to his marriage. What had happened between him and Meredith Lloyd? Was it so painful that he had found it necessary to retreat from the very cultural centers that creative people normally found stimulating? Why was his public persona so very different from the way he behaved in private?

If the journalist in Rachel wanted the answers, the woman in her was reluctant to make them public. It was all very well to storm up to New Hampshire intent on revenge against a man she had never met, but now she had met him, and liked him, and found him much too attractive for her own good. If his book had caused her pain at least he hadn't known her personally at the time he had written it. At the moment her inclination was to first deliver the blistering dressing-down he richly deserved and then to put *A Latin American Tragedy* behind her.

But Rachel's curiosity ultimately overrode every other consideration when it came to deciding her next move. If she confronted Jason now she might never learn the answers to all her questions about him. Certainly he wasn't going to confide the story of his life to *her* when he had heretofore refused to make even the briefest of personal comments to far cleverer interviewers. She would be in New Hampshire for a whole month and would use the time to find out everything she could about him. The inevitable showdown could wait.

Her feelings, while far more positive than they had been twenty-four hours before, were still confused. She was certain of only two things. First, there would be no affair with Jason Wilder. Her marriage to Carlos had left her with the realization that she would need love and commitment from a man before going to bed with him. If Jason wanted her it was only because she was a beautiful, challenging woman. Unfortunately for him, Rachel considered casual sex to be an empty exercise. She wasn't interested in it.

The second thing Rachel was sure of was that if she had any sense at all she would take advantage of the beauty and peacefulness of New Hampshire to get herself a thorough rest. She would be returning to her hectic life in New York soon enough, after all. The only problem, she thought with a wry smile, was that she would probably die of boredom by the end of the first week.

# Chapter Five

On Sunday afternoon two widowed sisters who had been girlhood friends of Lady Bennett's arrived for a five-day visit. Ethel Sarandon and Abby O'Dell had grown up in the same Boston suburb as Olivia McKay Wilder Bennett. Each had subsequently married, moved into her own home with her new husband and borne children, but all of them had remained close to each other until Lady Bennett's remarriage took her to England. Since that time the sisters and Lady Bennett had kept in touch primarily through sporadic letters. This visit marked the first time in over fifteen years that all three of them had been together.

Their presence had little effect on Rachel's routine. Since Mrs. Sarandon's arthritic back precluded horseback riding she was able to go riding each morning with Lady Bennett and Mrs. O'Dell. Her mount was Chescka, the gentle mare she had made friends with on Saturday.

Afterward she fixed everyone breakfast. All three women ate lightly—fruit, toast and coffee, with an occasional poached egg. Jason, who never joined them in the dining room, typically wanted something more substantial. He appeared to have so little interest in the specifics that after Sunday morning Rachel stopped going upstairs for his order and simply cooked him whatever struck her fancy. Since Synge had taken to trailing her around she was reasonably certain that he wasn't the recipient of her beautiful Spanish omelets.

As Jason had requested, Rachel also brought up a light lunch each day. The first few times she was alone with him she was careful to seem businesslike and respectful. When there were no more provocative comments or appraising stares, however, she gradually relaxed, her manner warming slightly to impersonal friendliness.

She supposed that Jason was wholly absorbed in his novel, a love story set against the background of a fictional Middle East war. Since Rachel's bed was almost directly underneath his desk, many nights she fell asleep to the sound of his typewriter. The noise never bothered her.

As far as she could discover, Jason left his office only twice each day: in mid-afternoon, to exercise himself and his horse, and in the early evening, to join everyone in the dining room. As a result, the only time Rachel really spoke with him was at dinner.

She was enjoying her job as chef to Lady Bennett and her guests. She had much more freedom working in a private home than she had ever had as a caterer; one's creativity was necessarily limited when cooking for large groups and exacting employers. In contrast, the choice of menus in New Hampshire was entirely her own, and since she liked to experiment with new recipes her selections were eclectic—country French one night, northern Italian the next, Mexican the third.

Everything she cooked met with enthusiastic reception. Even Jason, who initially seemed eager to rush back up to his work, soon told her that he looked forward to lingering over dinner every night. This compliment to Rachel's culinary skill was accompanied by a rueful glance at his waistline, which showed absolutely no sign of his supposed overindulgence.

From the beginning Rachel had felt as much a guest as an employee in this house, and thus didn't hesitate to accept Lady Bennett's invitation to join her and her guests at the table. Meals were informal. Although the three older women invariably changed from slacks into casual dresses each evening, Jason came downstairs in his usual blue jeans and sport shirt, the long sleeves of the latter either buttoned at the cuffs or rolled up, depending on the weather.

His clothing looked incongruous in this room, the Chinoiserie wallpaper and brocade-covered eighteenth century armchairs at war with the twentieth century denim. But when Lady Bennett scolded him about it he merely reminded her that although he had chosen to live in a house furnished with museum-quality antiques he had no intention of turning into one himself. As for Rachel, she was in and out of the kitchen so often that her own jeans and blouses were presumably considered necessary work clothes.

Jason was an unusual mixture of the formal and the casual, a lack of consistency which Rachel found attractive. In her experience with the talented and wealthy she had observed that the type of person who chose to surround himself with Georgian elegance did not customarily pad shoeless down to the dinner table. This same dichotomy existed in Jason's books, and even in his speech, which was wittily polished at one moment then smoothly altered to idiomatic American the next.

He had the self-assurance of those who are born to wealth and influence. Rachel couldn't imagine him uneasy or out of place, no matter what the situation. His behavior at these evening meals was impeccable. If at times he was itching to insert a mordant comment or dry retort, he didn't indulge himself. Lady Bennett's friends, well-meaning but simple, would not have understood.

They talked of books and plays, of work and family, and reminisced in the innocuous manner of childhood friends with little in common anymore. Their mutual history was of special interest to Rachel because it provided some insight into Jason's background. The challenge was to understand him in light of events which had taken place thirty or more years before.

In answer to one of Rachel's questions Lady Bennett explained that Jason's father was descended from a long line of New Englanders, the first Wilder having arrived in Massachusetts in the late 1600s. Among them were attorneys, judges and political leaders. The antiques in the house were a reflection

of that heritage; most of them were family heir-
looms. Given their quailty, Rachel realized, Jason
could not have purchased them himself. Even a
millionaire would have been compelled to file for
bankruptcy before furnishing half the downstairs.

As for Lady Bennett's background, she was the
daughter of a businessman and the granddaughter of
a politician. She had been strong-willed even as a
girl, eager for a career as a ballerina. World War II
had intervened; the talented young classical dancer
had volunteered to work as a chorus girl in a USO
show, thinking that the job would be only a temporary one.

The McKay family had always been friendly with
the Wilders, but, because of the difference in age
between their respective offspring, Olivia McKay
had never met Julian Wilder until he sought her out
after a performance to convey his parents' regards.
An attorney twelve years her senior, he had interrupted his career to serve in the military. They were
married within a month.

"And that was the end of my career," Lady
Bennett concluded. "Julian was very proper, Rachel, very much the master of the house. In his
world, women were wives and mothers. One might
say that he channeled my talents as a dancer into
suitable charity productions. I accepted it because I
adored him utterly—even idolized him. I wanted to
please him. Nonetheless, when I remarried, I quite
consciously chose a different sort of man. Ronny is
far more of a free spirit. Not a stuffy archaeologist at
all. He encouraged Jason with his acting—helped
arrange for all that marvelous English classical training he had—whereas Julian would have disinherited
him."

Jason sat and listened, making no comment about either his father or his stepfather. He seemed to find family history far less objectionable than a number of other topics, particularly rhapsodies on what an adorable, towheaded toddler he had been. Unfortunately, that particular subject was Abby O'Dell's very favorite.

"Do you remember," she asked Lady Bennett Tuesday night, "when you and Julian gave that dinner party for the mayor? And Jason's nanny was giving him his bath and got shampoo in his eyes? He came running downstairs, Rachel, howling at the top of his lungs, soaking wet and stark naked!"

She looked at Jason, who was focusing on his veal in an apparent attempt to disguise his impatience with yet another of her stories. "You soaked the mayor's suit and got shampoo in his consomme. He had no great liking for children, dear, especially after *you* finished up with him!"

Ethel Sarandon, more sensitive to her host's mood than her garrulous sister, caught his wan smile and promptly changed the subject. "Rachel, dear," she began, "are you the same 'Rachel Grant' who writes for all those magazines?"

Rachel glanced at Jason, noting the momentary surprise in his eyes, and then nodded. Thus diverted, Abby O'Dell immediately began to question Rachel about her work. Three and a half years as a caterer had given her a wealth of material to draw on so she was able to amuse everyone with anecdotes about eccentric or difficult clients, tactfully naming no names. Her articles, she explained, were generally written on assignment now, with story ideas coming from both editors and herself.

She was surprised by Jason's subsequent failure to

cross-examine her, if only out of curiosity about a fellow writer. Instead, he continued to leave her strictly alone, his manner devoid of any personal interest.

At dinner the next night he obliged his mother's guests with a long discourse on the political background of his current novel. Rachel knew that if he had done even half that much research on Santandian society there would have been no way he could have failed to remember that Raquel Garcia Martinez was the daughter of former American ambassador Thomas Grant. Yet he gave absolutely no sign of recognition.

Had Rachel taken Jason at face value she would have labeled him as an intelligent man of considerable charm and even temperament who had a high degree of tolerance for foolishness or dullness in his companions. Furthermore, she would have had reason to assume that he quickly lost interest in all but the easiest of sexual conquests; certainly he no longer displayed any of the open desire which had troubled and annoyed her on her first day in New Hampshire.

But Rachel was playing two roles, that of investigative reporter as well as a cook, and the portrait she received from others was that of a complex, inconsistent man, capable of generosity and love, guilty of thoughtlessness and perverse humor. In spite of the one-sided picture she received personally, she soon started to think of him as a fellow human being rather than as either the unfeeling author of *Tinseltown* and *A Latin American Tragedy* or as the lover of her fantasies.

Her most valuable source of information was Karen Rideau, the housekeeper whom Lady Bennett had termed "a sweet little thing." The description was entirely apt. Karen, who came in to do the cleaning and laundry two days a week, was twenty-four years old, petite and pretty, anxious to please and energetic. She thought that Jason Wilder was not only the most brilliant man she had ever met, but also one of the kindest. She admitted that he was subject to fits of cutting ill-humor, however, and warned Rachel to steer clear of him when he was in what she called "one of his moods."

Over a cup of coffee on Tuesday morning she told Rachel about the time she had come in to clean and found that Jason hadn't fixed himself his usual substantial breakfast. "I offered to make him something to eat, but he said he wasn't hungry. The truth is, I don't think he likes my cooking. Anyway, I could see he was in the middle of writing, so I went downstairs to do the laundry. I never should have nagged him about lunch."

"But you did," Rachel said with a smile, making mental notes on the conversation. There was a journal locked in her suitcase. It contained a description of everything she had learned, right down to the direct quotations she carefully entered each day.

"I was making myself a tuna fish sandwich, so I made him one too. I brought it upstairs and he said he didn't want it. I shouldn't have said what I did, but I'm so used to telling my little boys . . ."

Karen's face was a dusky red by now. "I marched over and put it on top of his typewriter and said, 'You have to eat, Mr. Wilder. It's not good to go without food,' and he totally lost his temper. I mean, there wasn't even any warning. He just blew up. He took the plate and threw it right across the room. The china went one way and the sandwich went the other way. Synge was sleeping in the den up there and he came bounding in . . ."

"I've already noticed he has a sixth sense about food," Rachel said.

"I was stammering an apology and saying I would clean up the mess and Mr. Wilder ended up ordering both of us to leave. His language was awful. After that, I thought I'd never come back again, but he called the next day to say he was sorry he yelled at me, that he was upset about something else and that it wouldn't happen again. I learned my lesson, though. I try not to nag him anymore, even though I think he should work less and eat more. I just bring him a sandwich and if he doesn't want it, that's his business. And I stay away from him when he's grouchy. I was pretty new back then, but now I can spot one of his moods a lot better. He hasn't screamed at me since, but the looks he can give you are almost as bad."

Rachel would never have destroyed the girl's illusions by telling her that Synge was the ultimate recipient of her thoughtfulness. She explained that Lady Bennett shared her concern and added that Jason now accepted the light lunches she brought him each afternoon. "I tempt him with homemade bread and fancy ingredients and he hasn't thrown anything at me yet."

Karen immediately assumed that Rachel, like herself, had Jason Wilder's best interests at heart. She was only too eager to discuss him after that, but it was obvious to Rachel that she looked upon him almost as a god. First of all, the books he wrote were hard for her to understand because of the complex ideas he presented and the vocabulary he used. To Karen, that marked him as a genius. Second, he had arranged for a slew of specialists to treat her husband, flown Paul Rideau down to Boston in his private plane and helped Karen pay the bills, actions which marked him as a great humanitarian. Karen so idolized him that his occasional human failings—snappish moods, a tendency to withdraw, impatience with imperfection, even thrown dishes—were taken as proof of artistic brilliance.

Rachel learned from Karen that one of the many doctors who had treated Paul Rideau was her brother-in-law, Philip Lenglen, another of those odd coincidences which seemed to tie Rachel's life to Jason Wilder's. Although Philip had gone to Boston to study with a team of plastic surgeons famed for pioneering methods of correcting genetic facial deformities, he accepted other types of cases as well. The skin grafts on Paul's face and upper body were examples of his handiwork and Karen was thrilled with the final results.

Rachel was too thorough and methodical not to exploit all possible sources of information. The daily routine she soon established included a morning trip to town, where she usually dropped in on Mr. Pepper, the librarian, and Mr. and Mrs. DeFalco, the grocers. She knew it was inefficient to shop every day, but was more concerned with filling up her time than with saving gasoline. An active woman accustomed to the harried pace of New York life, Rachel was finding it difficult to adjust to New Hampshire. Her job up here had turned into the vacation Lady Bennett had promised and, just as Rachel had feared, several times a day it was necessary for her to grit her teeth and remind herself how lucky she was to have obtained such a sinecure.

It was simple for her to convince the DeFalcos and

Mr. Pepper that she was smitten with Jason Wilder and wished only to please him. She had only to mention to Enos Pepper that Jason had asked her to pick him up something light to read and then agonize endlessly over the choice of a book. They wound up having a forty-five minute conversation about Jason Wilder and although at first the topic was his taste in best sellers, within twenty minutes Rachel had expertly broadened the subject matter.

Enos Pepper was only too willing to tell her all about Jason's research methods, not all of them standard uses of secondary and source materials. "And the fact is, he charms them into saying more than they mean to," he noted toward the end of the conversation. Rachel had no doubt that the people Mr. Pepper referred to were female. "You be careful what you say to him, Miss." This last comment, though delivered deadpan, was obviously meant as a joke.

The next time they talked Mr. Pepper had warmed to the point of telling Rachel about the time that Jason had agreed to come to the library to address the Linwood Writers Club. Half the surrounding area had shown up, but what they wanted to hear about was his movies, not his writing.

"Spun a bunch of tales for them, he did," Mr. Pepper told her. "Gullible fools. Believed all that rot about dangerous stunts and jealous husbands coming after him. At the end of it he looked around the room real slow and told them they'd just taken a class in how to write popular fiction. 'Just give the reader what he wants,' he said. And then he walked right out the door."

While condemning Jason for his lack of patience

Rachel found herself laughing at his sardonic sense of humor.

As for the DeFalcos, Rachel's initial question had to do with Jason Wilder's preferences in food. Originally from Brooklyn, they were far more loquacious than Enos Pepper and it was easier to draw them out. By Wednesday Mrs. DeFalco had taken Rachel aside to caution her not to become involved with Jason Wilder. Rachel's embarrassed admission about how attractive she found him, how brilliant, was met with dark warnings that he was a loner. It was not difficult to elicit information about the local hearts he had broken, his tastes in everything from coffee to women, the curiosity seekers he had forcibly ejected from his home and the famous friends who had come for three-day weekends.

Rachel was so absorbed in her research that she blithely rationalized her deception of these well-meaning people as both necessary and harmless.

Each day, after lunch, she packed her swimsuit, towel and writing materials into a canvas tote and went for a long walk. Synge, who loved to accompany her, could be counted on to rescue her if she got lost in the woods, which she frequently did. Eventually they would make their way to the lake, where Rachel rowed and sunbathed. She also wrote a daily letter to Susan, relating what was happening in New Hampshire in as much detail as she could manage on the aerogram forms she used. Writing down her feelings, she found, accomplished absolutely nothing in the way of clarifying them.

In addition, she was working on the article she owed to *Homemaker Magazine,* and by Thursday had finished a final longhand draft. Since Jason was by now aware of her career as a free-lance writer she went up to his office late the same afternoon and asked if she could use his typewriter for a few hours.

He lazed back in his chair, studying her for several seconds before drawling at her, "Do I get something in return?"

It was the first personal comment he had made all week, and though his tone was not precisely lecherous, it had a needling quality to it that made Rachel both uncomfortable and angry. "You get my thanks," she answered coolly.

He shook his head. "Not good enough. I need some recreation, Rachel." He paused just long enough to make sure that she had misinterpreted that statement, then continued, "Beat me in hockey and you can use the typewriter."

He wasn't interested in hockey so much as in victory, Rachel sensed. He was merely transposing his desire for conquest onto a different battlefield.

She certainly wasn't about to let him destroy her composure over some adolescent game, so she quickly accepted the challenge. Unfortunately, she never stood a chance. He totally demolished her, repeatedly slamming the puck into the edges of the miniature table-top field to carom straight into the goal she was attempting to defend. Even more galling, he consistently toyed with her, permitting her an occasional shot at his goal, then expertly blocking it.

Every time he scored or she failed to, Rachel's temper heated up a little more. She knew he wanted to break through her cool façade and because she was competitive enough to hate losing so badly he ultimately succeeded. "It's not fair!" she burst out at the end of the game. "You've played this thing a million times. How can I ever beat you?"

"Practice." His face was expressionless. "Two out of three, Rachel?"

There was a certain mocking triumph behind that bland tone of his which goaded Rachel into snapping at him, "If you need recreation, go ride your horse!"

"Space fighters?" he asked with a grin.

"No."

"Baseball, then," he cajoled. "Come on, Rachel."

His voice was so hopefully boyish that Rachel's irritation gave way to laughter. "You're impossible!" she said. "And very bossy. Are you going to show me how to use the typewriter or aren't you?"

"*I'm* bossy? You've been living here less than a week and you're already telling me what to do." He draped a casual arm over her shoulder and started toward his office.

Rachel, annoyed by the presumption of possession in his gesture, stiffened and removed herself from his embrace.

He stopped walking. "Sorry, Rachel. My mind was somewhere else," he murmured.

Rachel had no idea what to make of this distracted apology. They continued into the office, where he gave her a five-minute demonstration of the typewriter, told her he had some errands to run and then left her alone.


Abby O'Dell and Ethel Sarandon departed after dinner on Thursday and were replaced on Friday by two English couples, friends of Lady Bennett's who had been vacationing together in Canada. All four of her guests were connected with the English theater, their occupations obviously no coincidence given their hostess's plans for her son. Jason seemed to be interested in their work, but turned aside questions about his refusal to return to the stage with the smiling explanation that he had a publishing deadline to meet.

At times Rachel saw a wistful softness in his eyes or heard an eagerness in his voice that hinted at a love of performing, but in general the dinner conversation sounded more like a critics' convention than anything else. They talked of the latest plays on both sides of the Atlantic, Jason far more familiar with both the commercial and avant garde theater than Rachel had expected him to be. Having seen many of the New York productions under discusssion she didn't hesitate to offer her opinions and forcefully argue her point of view. When she and Jason disagreed the sexual electricity that charged the air had nothing to do with the topic under discussion. But there was no prospect of relief. After dinner each night Jason would excuse himself with a polite good-night and then closet himself in his office.

Lunchtime games of hockey and baseball only added to the tension between them. Rachel had decided that Jason's victory on Thursday had been a way of demonstrating his dominance over her. It hadn't been enough for him to win—he had wanted to crush her, to control the game so totally that even her attacks were subject to his whim. His subjugation of her, although entirely metaphorical, made her long for revenge.

By Friday she was itching for a rematch and, even more than that, determined to get under his skin the way he'd gotten under hers. Her first move was to suggest a game of video baseball because he couldn't control the play as he had with table hockey.

"Sure," he said. Rachel could have kicked him for his bored tone, but gave no sign of her feelings. "But don't feel bad if I cream you."

Although he easily beat her, at least she had the satisfaction of doing much better in the rematch. "Hockey?" he invited afterward.

Rachel ignored his superior smile. "Sure." She congratulated herself on sounding just as bored as he had earlier. She wasn't going to let him goad her into losing her temper—not *this* time.

In fact, he routed her so unmercifully that for the first half of the game she had to clench her teeth to keep from yelling at him. And then a better strategy suggested itself.

She knew all about the screenplay in Jason's head. Arouse her anger and all her other defenses were supposed to crumble. They would go from angry words to a physical tussle to a passionate embrace on his bed.

*Not if I have anything to say about it!* she thought. From that point on, whenever she was alone with Jason, she adopted a manner so respectfully distant that it was a taunt in itself. Every other sentence she spoke ended with "Mr. Wilder." She permitted no real conversation between them, never again lost her temper and showed absolutely no personal interest in him.

He didn't seem to notice that her behavior was anything out of the ordinary, but Rachel wasn't fooled by his pretended nonchalance. He was so coldly determined to win every game that he had to be using victory as compensation for her recalcitrance. Rachel was irresistibly drawn to the idea of courting danger. Although she continued to insist to herself that she had no intention of becoming involved with Jason Wilder she found it wildly exciting to continually provoke him. She didn't suppose she was fooling him any more than he was fooling her. Eventually, she knew, he was going to lose patience with children's games and make a very adult move. What she didn't know was how she would react to it.

## *Chapter Six*

On the second Tuesday of Rachel's stay in New Hampshire she received a pair of letters from Susan which, though written and mailed several days apart, had nonetheless arrived in Linwood at the same time. The first was full of enthusiasm for the trip ahead and mentioned that she and Sarah had met two young professors, both of whom taught in California, on the plane to Paris. The four of them had decided to travel together, following the rough outline of Susan's itinerary. Susan evidently looked upon the men only as escorts who would make their vacation somewhat safer, but Rachel quickly realized that one or both of them might become romantically interested in her sister. She hoped so; it would do no harm for Susan to realize that there were other men in the world besides Dr. Philip Lenglen.

The second letter seemed to grant her wish much too completely. Susan had a great deal to say about one of her male companions, a history teacher named Kenny. He was apparently no less interested in Susan than she was in him, but since he lived in California the relationship could have no future. Rachel feared that that was precisely its appeal to him, if not to her sister. There was no doubt that Susan still loved Philip, but eighteen months without him had left her ripe for experimentation. Unfortunately, she had absolutely no experience with light-hearted affairs. She might easily become far more involved than she intended, only to be badly hurt when it was over.

Rachel took the two letters to the lake with her, wondering what sort of answer she should send. Susan seemed to want her advice, but in this particular instance Rachel could only caution her to take her time about taking a lover. "You can always say 'yes' later," she wrote. "Enjoy the attention you're getting, but don't let him push you into something you're not ready for. *You* have to decide what *you* want."

The rest of the letter, composed as she lay on a beach towel in her bathing suit, was concerned primarily with her changing emotions toward Jason. "I don't know why I provoke him," she admitted toward the end of the letter. "I suppose that part of me wishes he'd put a stop to the game we've been playing, maybe by hauling me off to bed. The waiting is agony. It bothers me that I'm so passive when I'm usually the opposite, but maybe I'm afraid to care for him because of who he is. I don't think of him as only the 'author' Jason Wilder anymore, but even so, it seems hopelessly neurotic that I, of all people, should become involved with him. Anyway, enough of my confused emotions. As for yours, I hope you'll be careful."

She paused a moment, realizing that her warning might well be too late. Perhaps Susan should spend a week or two in New Hampshire when she got back to the States so that she and Rachel could talk about everything that had happened. Since Lady Bennett's original offer had applied to both of them there would be no objections from that quarter. Nonetheless, she was living in Jason's house and was nominally his employee. She would have to check with him first.

The opportunity presented itself sooner than she had expected. She was lying on her back, knees bent, a hand flung across her eyes to block out the sun, when the sound of a body hitting the water broke into her thoughts. Rachel assumed it was Synge—the dog had a habit of paddling around in the lake, trotting right up to her and then shaking himself with such vigor that half the pond wound up on her skin. A lazy glance to the side revealed that Jason was the one responsible for the splash. He was swimming across the lake, having tethered Caligula to a tree on the opposite shore. His clothing was strewn on the ground some distance away from the restless horse.

Rachel sat up, instinctively pulling at the top of her strapless black and white maillot. Jason touched bottom and strode to the shore, water streaming from his body, his hand brushing the wet hair from his eyes. He was wearing a pair of navy shorts in lieu of a swimsuit; they clung to his hips, presenting such a godlike picture that Rachel wound up staring at him with uncharacteristic detachment. She might have looked at a particularly beautiful piece of sculpture in much the same way. She had seen as much of his bare skin on movie screens as she did now, of course, but reality was more compelling than celluloid. He looked handsome, powerful and arrogantly male.

He smiled at the expression on her face. "A sex object all over again," he drawled. "And here I wanted you to respect me for my mind."

Rachel got up, handing him the towel she had been sitting on. "You really are magnificent," she said, sounding analytical rather than admiring. "What does it feel like to know there are millions of women who wish you'd strip for the camera again?"

"Annoying. Frustrating. I wanted to play Hamlet, not get my clothes ripped off by a crazed kangaroo in heat." His wry reference was to one of the enemy aliens in the movie *Parallel Universe* and Rachel had to smile at the aptness of his metaphor.

They hadn't exchanged so many meaningful sentences in all their many hours of game-playing and Rachel had no desire to start fencing with him again. "Is that why you stopped making movies?" she asked. "Because you felt stereotyped?"

"Partly. All-American looks can be a liability when it comes to getting interesting parts." He handed her the now-damp towel, which she spread on the grass. "You come here every day, don't you?"

Rachel accepted the change of subject without comment, only too aware that neither of them wore very many clothes. Her appreciation of his appearance was far more than aesthetic by now.

"Every day," she agreed. "To lick my wounds after you demolish me in one of your games."

Remembering the frustrated admission of passivity in her letter to Susan, she forced herself to continue, "You do it to punish me, don't you? Because I haven't fallen into bed with you yet."

"Would I do any better with you if I let you win?" he asked teasingly.

"You know what I mean," Rachel answered.

"You're right. I know what you mean. But if punishment is what we're discussing, you're better at inflicting it than I am. The colder you act, the more it frustrates me. Believe it or not, I don't get much of a kick out of dominating you. Not after the first time, anyway."

"What was so special about the first time?"

"You lost your temper. Now you don't, no matter how angry I make you. I'd say that makes you the winner."

His admission of defeat softened her attitude, although she herself would have called the situation a standoff. "Truce?" she offered.

He smiled. "I thought I'd just surrendered." He glanced at the blue aerogram sitting by her tote bag. "Who are you writing to?"

"My younger sister. She's in France for two weeks. Would you mind if she came up here when she gets back?"

"Not at all. I'd like to meet her." He sounded as though he meant this conventional reply.

"You know her husband—Philip Lenglen, the plastic surgeon who worked on Karen's husband. He and Suzy have been separated for the past eighteen months."

"Tell me about it."

Rachel did so, with an openness that surprised both of them. Ordinarily she was worse than tight-lipped about family matters, but she discovered that Jason Wilder's subtle prompting made it extraordinarily easy for her to confide in him.

When she finished he told her that the story hadn't particularly surprised him. "It's second nature to me by now to size people up. Then they seem to find their way into my books. Lenglen's the type who becomes personally involved with his patients—I could see it with Paul. Based on what you've told me, it may be a substitute for lasting relationships, a safe outlet for his emotions. Once the patient is cured, his responsibility can end. The commitment is self-limiting."

"Then why did he want Suzy to give up her job?"

"I'd say that, unconsciously, he wanted to drive her away. He knew she'd refuse to do what he wanted. But instead of giving up or leaving, she tried to work things out. So he had an affair and that accomplished his goal."

Rachel, finding the explanation inconsistent, asked, "Then why marry her in the first place? Why give that kind of commitment?"

"Probably because he was very much in love with her and didn't want to lose her. Ten to one he rationalized the demand that she give up her career by telling himself that he wanted to keep her close to him. He can even justify the affair by thinking that he went to another woman for the attention your sister wasn't giving him. Look at his behavior. He alternately pushes her away and pulls her back. He didn't have to go to Boston to study. There must be doctors in New York he could have worked with. It was far, but not too far. Same with the phone calls. He can't stand letting her go, but like you said, he's scared to let her get too close. You'd have to ask him why that is."

"Suzy and her friend are traveling with a couple of college teachers," Rachel told him. "I think she may be involved with one of them."

"I'd like to get your sister, her boyfriend, and her husband up here and study them for a while. This has the makings of a good novel," Jason remarked with a wink.

Rachel almost blurted out, "Not two from the same family!" but caught herself in time. Jason was pointing to the boat, asking Rachel to join him. "I feel like rowing. Come keep me company."

When both of them were seated she asked him why he wasn't up in his office working, her mind more on the way his arm muscles rippled as he pulled the oars through the water than on whatever answer he might give.

"I could lie and say 'writer's block,' but I won't. I came to find you, to talk to you. I told you you needed to know me better and I've given you ten days to do it in. But you haven't made much of an effort. That game we were playing was driving me crazy, Rachel. I can't take another day of it. How long are you going to keep me waiting?"

Rachel hadn't expected the conversation to take such an abrupt personal turn. "I told you, Jason," she said, "if I want to sleep with you . . ."

"Do you realize that that's the first time you haven't 'Mr. Wildered' me?" he interrupted, smiling at her. "Relax. I'm not going to pounce on you."

"I didn't think you were." The drawled denial was automatic, a testament to four years of fending off passes from hot-blooded New York wolves.

"Yet," he began lightly, then continued in a more serious tone, "you asked me why I stopped making movies. It wasn't just the stereotyping. The roles were there—a few of them. Maybe I wasn't convincing enough, not a good enough actor."

Rachel was aware that he had returned to the subject of his career out of a sensitivity to her dislike of the previous topic. She shook her head. "You don't believe that," she said.

"No, you're right. I don't. I think it was hopeless. It's part of the reason I stopped making films. I looked like the guy in the white hat and that's how people always saw me. I can't blame them. In three successive movies I saved the solar system, the galaxy, and the whole damn universe. Meanwhile, my relationship with Meredith was going to hell. I wrote *Tinseltown* out of sheer perversity. I wanted to be hated instead of loved."

Half a dozen interviewers would have sold their souls to be sitting where Rachel was. When Jason wanted someone to "know him better," she decided, he didn't fool around. "What happened?" she asked aloud.

"When I met Meredith Lloyd she was one of the hottest stars on T.V. and I was a nobody, acting with a rep company in Los Angeles. I was totally infatuated with her. I asked her to marry me on our second date, and our third and our fourth. It wasn't only physical. Meredith was bright and talented, and selfish in a way that I was too inexperienced to recognize. She seemed vulnerable and unsure of herself and it made me want to take care of her—to show her how special she was. Of course, those qualities had the same effect on her fans—they made her into a star. She finally said 'yes' when I was chosen for the lead in *Parallel Universe*."

He pulled in the oars, letting the boat drift slowly on the water. "She loved me as long as I worshipped her. She liked my success—at first. It turned her on . . . to possess a man other women wanted. Unfortunately, it also threatened her. The more successful I became the less time I had to cater to her. And I admit I started to expect some care and affection back, but it didn't work that way with Meredith. She was a taker who had to be number one. And when she wasn't anymore, she felt betrayed."

"Are you talking about when her show got cancelled?" Rachel asked.

"In part. You have to understand that her vulnerability wasn't entirely an act. She really *was* insecure. She felt unloved as a child, which was perfectly rational, given the lousy parents she had. She spent her adult life trying to compensate for it. The devotion of an audience can be a workable substitute for feeling good about yourself. The only problem is that fans are notoriously fickle. Meredith was 'this year's redhead' for four straight years and then she got replaced by 'this year's blonde.' She made a movie and it flopped, and she felt totally abandoned. By then the photographers were trailing around after me instead of her, and that made her jealous of me, angry with me. The fact that I'm uncomfortable with crowds and publicity only made it worse. I had something she wanted and I didn't even like it." He paused for a moment, then went on, "I tried to be supportive, to tell her there would be other roles, to convince her she had a lot going for her. She didn't want to hear that—it was easier to feel sorry for herself. She even accused me of patronizing her. I have to admit that she chose a brilliant method of retaliation—self-destructive and painful to me, all at once."

Rachel didn't prompt him. His eyes had dropped to his lap, but not before she caught the look in them. Whatever Meredith Lloyd had done, it still hurt years later. Jason started to row again, taking the boat toward the feeder stream.

"I wanted children. We'd talked about it when we got married, but I accepted the fact that a pregnancy would interrupt Meredith's career. And later on, when I realized the problems we had, I knew that having children under those circumstances would be a mistake. That was when Meredith became pregnant—and told me that she wasn't going to have the baby." He stared across at Rachel. "Abortion was something I *couldn't* accept—not *my* child. I told her I would raise it, and she went into a tirade about how pregnancy would ruin her body. So finally I asked her why she even told me about it if she'd already decided to have an abortion. She just looked at me. Didn't say a word."

He laughed, a short, bitter snort of a sound. "You should have seen the triumph in her eyes. I started yelling at her and she slammed out of the house. She stayed out all night, which was probably just as well because I felt like killing her. The next day she walked onto the set where I was filming and told me that she had, quote, unquote, gotten rid of your brat.

"What was left of our marriage fell apart after that. Meredith started to sleep around and so did I.

She got pregnant again—someone else's kid this time; I hadn't touched her in over two months. And she told me she was keeping the baby. By then, I shouldn't have cared, but I did."

The pain in his eyes was so real to Rachel that she actually felt it rising in her own throat. "You can't imagine what it did to me. It tore at my guts, just like she knew it would. I've never come so close to beating a woman up. You know the rest. Everyone does. She went on location to Arizona to shoot a T.V. movie and ended up dead in her co-star's bed. I blamed Hollywood for destroying her and went on a whole guilt trip because my own success had contributed to it. It took me months to put things into perspective, to realize that I'd tried to help her. Eventually I accepted the fact that Meredith was responsible for her own life—and death. You've heard my mother mention Stephen Chapin. He was there at a time when I needed a good friend, which makes it doubly hard to say no to him now. But I just don't want to act again. I've had enough of being a celebrity."

Rachel's eyes conveyed the empathy she felt. She knew something about pain herself, enough to realize that the questions she might have asked would seem insensitive, that the comments she might have made would seem trite. She looked away, fixing her gaze on Caligula, who was grazing with that deceptive placidity of his. Jason brought the boat in to the shallows, jumped out and dragged it ashore. Rachel followed, still silent.

Jason's towel lay on the ground next to his shirt and shoes; he picked it up and spread it out on top of the pine needles. Then he sat down. Rachel hesitated before joining him. She knew what was coming. If she didn't want him to make love to her, she should get back in the boat and row across the lake.

Jason looked up at her, holding her eyes, and continued to talk. "I told you I wrote *Tinseltown* out of perversity. It was a way of mocking my own image, maybe even of punishing myself. I knew people would think it was about Meredith and me. So I made Marty selfish and corrosive, a composite of the biggest louses in the business, a few of whom I've actually had the misfortune to work with. I suppose that's the way I felt about myself, at first. But it was a long time ago. I've come to terms with it."

The pain had faded from his face to be replaced by a look of undisguised desire. Rachel's defenses instinctively took over, making her response brittle. "What's the point of telling me all this? A unique way of talking me into bed?"

He looked away, defeated, not answering. Rachel felt guilty for the unnecessary sarcasm. Then he murmured, "I told you, I want you to know me better. I'm tired of playing games, Rachel."

"And if we sleep together, what happens then?"

"Whatever you want." He reached out to catch her hand, gently pulling her down. The physical contact burned through Rachel's body, mocking her uncertainty, and she sank to her knees, her heartbeat increasingly violent. Jason slipped a finger through the elastic band that held her ponytail in place and slowly pulled it off.

She let him ease her onto her back, wanting him to touch her. Then he covered her body with his own, supporting his weight on one elbow, his other hand playing with her loosened hair, lightly stroking her cheek, wandering to her lips. Rachel stared into his eyes, saw the hunger in them, felt him tremble. She was overwhelmed by the emotion this man obviously felt, aroused not only by the touch of his body but by his intense response to her. He lowered his head, his mouth nuzzling her neck and hair, relishing its freedom to explore. Her strapless top was pulled down to her waist, allowing him to caress her breasts at will.

Rachel put her hands on his shoulders and then slid them down his arms, enjoying the way his muscled flesh felt under her fingertips. She turned her head, seeking his lips, her mouth teased open by hard fleeting kisses that left her aching with desire. Only when she arched against him and moaned his name did he begin to satisfy the longing he had aroused.

Rachel had never felt such passion in a kiss, such tightly restrained hunger. It was like a leashed atomic reaction. His tongue probed her mouth, both dominating and giving pleasure, and his body moved on top of her, deliberate yet at the same time urgent. At first stunned, she slowly succumbed, winding her arms around his neck, kissing him with impatient passion, lost in her own physical reactions.

Her few thoughts were disjointed. He's creative, she thought, an actor, a writer. He feels things intensely. Gets emotionally involved. But how could he manage to act so cool when he felt like this? And then—I've never wanted a man so much in my life. If he stopped now, I'd beg him to start again.

She knew he wouldn't stop. By now they were both breathing heavily, the kiss no longer satisfying to either of them. When Jason twisted his body half onto the ground and pulled Rachel close against his side she understood the message he was sending her. He wouldn't rush her by going too fast or touching too freely. He would wait until she was ready to continue. When her hand moved to the waistband of his shorts and began to fumble with the metal catch she felt him take a deep breath. He buried his face in her neck, kissing her hair.

"Maria . . ." he moaned.

If there was any name guaranteed to make Rachel recoil with shock, Jason Wilder had just mumbled it. Her body stiffened with horror; she could manage only a strangled whisper. "What did you call me?"

He drew back, his eyes glazed, miles away. As he focused on her face and read the look in her eyes he muttered, "I said . . ." A dull flush rose up his neck and face. "I'm sorry, Rachel. I didn't mean . . ."

Rachel yanked away from him and rolled onto her other side so that her back was to him. Her hands were shaking as she pulled her swimsuit back into place. It wasn't just that he knew who she was— there was probably no way that he *couldn't* have known. It was the way he had used her. She was furious at her own stupidity, her failure to understand what was going on in his mind. Naturally a man didn't react so intensely to a woman he'd known only ten days—she should have guessed the reason for his explosive emotional response. But even more than that, she was hurt that Jason could be so callous. Even Carlos had never stooped so low as to use her as a surrogate for another woman. To Jason Wilder she wasn't even another woman. She was a character from his novel.

He had put Maria through a verbal paper shredder, his condemnation only too obvious. What kind of twisted kick could he get from making love to the woman who had inspired that sort of disdain?

Rachel ached for the self-control to walk away without a word, but even sitting up proved an effort. Shivering, she crossed her arms and hugged them to her defensively. "You're really sick, you know that?" she said hoarsely.

"I'm sorry," he repeated. "You're not like Maria —not anymore. I wouldn't want you if you were. You've changed so much in four years that I didn't realize who you were . . . at first."

Rachel twisted around, meaning to glare at him, but there was more anguish than anger in her eyes. "Am I supposed to thank you for that—for your approval? What the hell did you think you were doing?"

"I could ask you the same question." Jason's voice was calmer now, much calmer than her own. "You came up here hating my guts—I felt it that first night and I've been getting flashes of it ever since. I suppose I can understand that. But if that's how you feel, why did you let me touch you today? Why did you *want* me to?"

"Because I'm a masochistic idiot," Rachel muttered, at that moment believing it to be true. If she hadn't unconsciously wanted punishment, why would she have subjected herself to the torment of getting involved with Jason Wilder?

"Look, can we talk this out?"

"We have nothing to say to each other." Rachel started to get up, only to have Jason catch her wrist to prevent her from leaving.

"That's baloney and you know it. You wouldn't have come up here unless you wanted to meet me. You knew who I was."

Stop running away, Rachel told herself. You think the man deserves to be told off, don't you? Well, here's the chance you've been waiting for.

She took a deep breath and let her wrist go limp. Jason released her as soon as he felt it slacken. "Yes, I knew who you were," she said with a soft fierceness, staring into her lap. "I've hated you for over a year. I worked very hard to get where I am, to put my marriage and my life in Latin America behind me. I thought I had become the kind of person I could respect. Your book ripped me apart so brutally that I began to doubt everything. I was depressed for months. If I hadn't had a good therapist, I might have ended up in a hospital."

"Rachel, it was fiction!" There was such agony in his voice that Rachel looked up at him in disbelief to find that the expression on his face matched the hoarseness of his tone. "It *was* based on you, and I talked to people—your husband's mistress, a few friends—I read the magazine articles, like everyone else . . ." He shook his head, as if unable to comprehend her accusation. "It was *fiction,* Rachel."

"It was my life," she replied, "right down to what went on in our bedroom."

The curse he muttered underscored not only his astonishment but his regret. It *couldn't* be an act, Rachel thought, at the same time doubting her instinct to trust him. She knew firsthand what an accomplished actor he was.

"I took what I knew about you and extrapolated," he insisted. "I wrote what I imagined you were like based on what I knew, a lot of research on the culture, my imagination. I had no idea how close I'd come, you have to believe that."

"Why should I? And if you'd known, would you have cared?" Rachel was far too angry to listen to explanations. "Did you ever stop to consider that there was a real person somewhere, a woman who might be hurt by your book?"

"You're right. Maybe if I'd met you—but I didn't. And it wouldn't have mattered." His tone was husky, rueful. "The situation obsessed me, Rachel. I *had* to write about it. I was furious with you—with Maria, I mean. She had beauty, intelligence, *potential*, damn it, and she threw it away on Antonio. How could you have let that slimy monster Garcia touch . . ." He stopped, silenced by the disgusted look on Rachel's face.

"You don't know *who* you mean!" she attacked.

"Okay, so I don't!" he exploded. "I didn't ask for all this. What do you think you're doing up here anyway? You think my mother invited you because she needed a *cook*?"

Rachel wasn't surprised to hear her suspicions about Lady Bennett's motivations confirmed. "No, I don't really think that. What does she want from me?"

"She knew who you were the minute Jackie Pollock mentioned your name. She'd met your father in Tokyo—my stepfather was on a lecture tour in Japan. It was just after *Tragedy* came out, so she started asking him about you—what you were doing with your life. She told me the story on Saturday when I confronted her about asking you up here. She thinks I'm vegetating, wasting my life, but you already know that. She came up with one hell of a way to shake me out of it, didn't she?"

"How could she know how you would react?"

"She knows how involved I was in the book. Don't be taken in by that dizzy English lady routine of hers. She's sharp as a tack and more perceptive than she'll admit. You impressed her. Hell, you'd impress anyone. She figured it would upset my equilibrium to meet you and she was dead right. I was too annoyed by her blasted invasion to notice much more than your hostility the night we met, but the next morning you seemed . . . familiar. I was too absorbed in other things to place you, even after I got the name straightened out. By that time, I wasn't particularly anxious to get rid of you—I was too attracted to you. Then I saw the way you looked at the books, and it clicked. It certainly explained your hostility to me. Now why don't *you* take a shot at explaining your ambivalence?"

Rachel was in no mood to bare her soul to this man. She settled on half the truth. "You're charming, handsome, perceptive and smart. I'm physically attracted to you, just like a hundred million other women. But I'm not getting involved with someone who thinks of me as the living embodiment of a character from some book."

"Every author's fantasy"—his tone was full of self-mockery—"taking his favorite heroine to bed. I worked on *Tragedy* for two years, loving Maria one moment, disgusted with her the next. You've realized all the potential I saw in her, Rachel. I look at you and I see all the parts I loved. I want you so much that I lie awake nights, thinking about you, telling myself I should be more patient."

"Listen to the way you talk. You don't even think of me as a real person."

"You're the same as Maria. You admitted it to me."

"I'm not!" Rachel said. "I've spent the last four years learning not to be. Be obsessed with her if that's what you want, but don't confuse us."

"Correction, then. You *were* Maria. But you can't just accept that and get on with your life, can you? That's where all that anger comes from. You're afraid you'll revert. That's why the book hit you so hard."

He was too perceptive; he understood her too well. "Look who's talking!" Rachel lashed back. "You had a neurotic obsession with Meredith, but even if she was sick, at least she was a real person. Now you're all hung up on a figment of your imagination. *You're* the one who needs a psychiatrist!"

His teeth were clenched together with repressed anger. "I think we've hurt each other enough for one day, Rachel," he growled, getting up. A minute later he was galloping away on his horse, still barechested and barefoot.

Rachel watched him disappear through the trees, then untied the boat and rowed back across the lake. The physical exercise calmed her anger. She had no right to be sanctimonious about this whole mess. After all, she had come to New Hampshire with her own hidden agenda, intending to do a hatchet job on Jason Wilder. When it came to compulsiveness, she was in the same league as he was. She hadn't had the slightest compunction about using Lady Bennett, Karen Rideau, Enos Pepper or anyone else who could provide her with information.

She had to admit that Olivia Bennett had set her

up with the consummate finesse of a professional con woman. If she had been confident that Rachel would accept her offer of a job it was because she had known all along that a piece of bait named Jason Wilder would prove to be irresistible.

As for Jason, Rachel couldn't stay angry with a man who acted more out of confusion than any Machiavellian depravity. She accepted the fact that he had thought he was writing fiction—that he genuinely had no idea that the character Maria bore an uncanny resemblance to the real-life Rachel. She understood that, at first, he had played along with her masquerade in an effort to gain the trust of someone he believed he loved, someone he perceived as hostile. Continual frustration and her own provocative behavior had subsequently goaded him into a display of taunting domination. But Rachel was convinced that the intense love he thought he felt was a fantasy, a neurotic obsession with a literary chimera.

And what of her own feelings? What did she want from Jason Wilder? She was coming to know an open, emotional man very different from any she had met before and she acknowledged his attractiveness. What she didn't know was whether that attraction would be so strong if he had been anyone other than the author of *A Latin American Tragedy*.

If she left New Hampshire her questions would never be answered. But if she stayed an affair with Jason was almost inevitable. At this point, he was far more emotionally involved than she was. When she thought about that she realized that there was now far more likelihood of her hurting him than the other way around.

She didn't want to do that. True, she had no desire

to lie in bed with him and hear him whisper passionate endearments to Maria, but she could survive it. It was far more upsetting to think of using Jason Wilder like some experimental animal, only to discard him if she found that her own feelings were nothing more than an illusion.

# Chapter Seven

$\mathcal{D}$inner that night was the most uncomfortable meal Rachel had ever suffered through. She had returned to the house late in the afternoon to be greeted by silence. Jason wasn't working in his office when she carried his clothing, towel and shoes upstairs; neither was there any sign of Lady Bennett, or a note as to her whereabouts. Most likely she was driving her guests to Lebanon airport for their flight to Boston, their next stop.

The next wave of the invasion was scheduled to arrive on Friday, when not only the Chapins but also the Pollocks would be driving up to Linwood. Unhappily for Lady Bennett the deployment of this heavy artillery—a producer, a playwright, an agent and Jackie Pollock, a regiment in and of herself—was ill-timed. Given Jason's mood when he had galloped off this afternoon Rachel didn't expect him to be particularly receptive to whatever arguments they mustered.

Since she had no idea whether she was cooking for one, two or three, she prepared a light meal that could be refrigerated for the next day's lunch: chilled strawberry soup, seafood crepes, and a tossed green salad. In fact, Jason and his mother returned to the house together, at about six-thirty, and immediately sat down to dinner. The silence was oppressive; even the normally vivacious Lady Bennett made no attempt to initiate conversation. About halfway through the meal Jason tossed his napkin on the table, stiffly thanked Rachel for dinner and then excused himself.

Rachel's mood had steadily worsened until she ached to do the same. She was troubled by the decision she had to make and impatient with the necessity of sitting politely at the table until Lady Bennett was finished with her meal.

"He's not in the best of moods today, is he?" Lady Bennett observed.

When Rachel merely shook her head in reply Lady Bennett went on, "But then, neither are you. Would it be intrusive of me to ask what happened?"

Rachel was sure that Lady Bennett had received at least a truncated account of the afternoon's events from her son. "Didn't he fill you in?" she asked. She knew she sounded waspish, but was not about to put up with a sly cross-examination at the hands of the woman sitting across from her.

"He's thirty-seven, Rachel. Don't you think he's a bit old to be confiding in Mama?" Lady Bennett settled back in her chair, waiting for Rachel's reaction.

Rachel's instinct was to snap out that, at age twenty-eight, she was a bit old for it, too. Since such a retort would have been unpardonably rude she merely took a few more bites of her sandwich and then pushed away her dish.

She was about to excuse herself to get the coffee when Lady Bennett remarked, "I believe I owe you an apology. It's quite clear to me that you had your own reasons for coming up here, but that hardly excuses my plotting, Rachel. I *am* sorry. My only excuse is that you seemed so thoroughly able to take care of yourself. It never occurred to me that you and Jason wouldn't talk it out straight away. But you finally did this afternoon, didn't you? Stopped tiptoeing around each other and acknowledged that each of you knew perfectly well who the other one was?"

Lady Bennett's sympathetic tone of voice shamed Rachel into an admission of her own. "I have no right to be angry at anyone, except maybe myself, for coming up here in the first place," she said. "At least your motive for asking me was to help your son although frankly, Olivia, I'm not sure he needs it. It's *his* life and he has good reasons for living it the way he does. My problem is where I go from here. I don't suppose it's going to solve anything to run away—not for either of us."

"Certainly not for Jason," Lady Bennett said, her angelic smile firmly in place. "He's quite besotted with you, Rachel. We're not asking him to change his whole way of life, you know, just to do a limited run of a single play. I believe you could convince him if you set your mind to it."

"You never give up, do you?" Rachel shook her head, smiling. As much as Lady Bennett's tone cajoled, it also mocked her own blithe single-mindedness.

"Usually not," she admitted. "But to be quite serious, in this instance I've gone a bit too far. The first day of our stay Jason tore into me about the whole business, furious about the position I'd put him in. He's passionate in his dislike of dishonesty and yet there he was, unable to tell you that he knew who you were for fear you'd up and leave. Naturally, he wants you to return his feelings and I'm very much in his corner. I met your father last year, in Tokyo; he was terribly proud of all you'd accomplished. With good reason, if I may say so. You've become an admirable young woman, Rachel."

Rachel felt so guilty in the wake of this tribute that further confession became a necessity. "Not so admirable. I came up her to write about him. I was bitter about the way the book had invaded my privacy and I wanted to give him a taste of the same thing."

"And will you?"

"No. As soon as he became a real person to me I knew I wouldn't do it. I suppose that revenge never accomplishes anything, except to make you feel worse about yourself."

Having purged her soul, Rachel was anxious to change the subject. She was groping for an innocuous topic when Lady Bennett exercised the tact of which she was so very capable and began to talk about Sir Ronald's latest expedition. The subject occupied them until the end of the meal.

As a young woman, Rachel had seldom considered either her motivations or the possible consequences of her actions. Especially since beginning therapy, however, she had learned to be analytical, perhaps too much so. As she cleaned up the kitchen she chided herself for not thinking through this uncharacteristically impulsive trip before charging up here. But even had she done so, she was forced to acknowledge, she never could have foreseen the situation she now found herself in.

She had expected Jason Wilder to be a cold cynic; instead she had discovered a man with the capacity for intense absorption and emotional involvement, qualities which helped make him both a fine actor and a compelling writer. It was illogical to expect that these same traits wouldn't carry over into his personal life. Raquel Garcia Martinez had, for some reason, fascinated him, angered him, even obsessed him. He had been involved with Rachel, through her literary analog Maria, long before the two of them ever actually met. Given the intensity of his feelings, she doubted he would be capable of examining them with any degree of distance or dispassion.

Trying to make sense of the situation, Rachel felt like a character in a Pirandello play who wanders through scene after scene, trying to distinguish illusion from reality. In her opinion, Jason really wanted the nonexistent Maria, but if he thought he wanted Rachel, or identified Rachel and Maria as the same person, didn't he for all practical purposes want Rachel too? Who was she to interpret his feelings, to tell him he didn't understand himself? At least he had a clear idea of what he would do, given the choice. That was far more than Rachel had.

By ten o'clock, having baked two cakes, abandoned a magazine article and taken Synge for a walk, Rachel ran out of ways to avoid the inevitable. On one level she was certain that talking with Jason would accomplish nothing—that their perceptions of this situation were so radically different that mutual understanding was impossible. On the other hand, there had to be a decision about what would happen next and she was not inclined to make it alone. Even had she been capable of doing so, it wouldn't have been fair to Jason.

She heard him typing as she climbed the steps to the attic. Not wanting to disturb him, she stood and watched for several minutes, waiting for him to take a break. The occasional pauses were so brief that Rachel wondered whether emotional turmoil provided him with inspiration. In unconscious answer to her question, he took the sheet of manuscript he had just completed and very deliberately tore it into strips, then watched the confettilike pieces waft to the floor.

"Jason?" Rachel called his name softly, prompting him to look back over his shoulder. His face was taut, his eyes guarded and cool.

"Can we talk?" she asked him. "I don't want to disturb you if you're in the middle of something."

He nodded toward the floor. "That's what I was in the middle of. Is the den all right? Or maybe you'd feel safer downstairs?"

Rachel ignored the taunt in his voice. "The den is fine."

The two of them proceeded next door, not speaking, taking the same seats as they had on the first day of Rachel's stay, Rachel on the love seat, Jason on the opposite couch. His attitude was just hostile enough to make her defensive, and she hesitated, wanting to choose her words carefully.

"You look nervous," Jason said. "Presumably a consequence of being alone with someone who's obsessive, neurotic and sick. What's on your mind, Rachel?"

Rachel quashed her impulse to lash back with similar sarcasm. She hadn't come up here to fight. "If you want me to leave New Hampshire," she said calmly, "you're certainly going about it the right way."

"You mean you're not packed yet?"

"Is that what you want me to do? Pack up and go?"

He looked away from her, obviously upset. "You know what I want."

Until that moment Rachel hadn't fully realized that Jason's sarcasm was an expression of pain rather than anger. "Jason, I'm sorry about the things I said," she told him. "I'm the last person in the world who should—"

"Why be sorry?" he interrupted. "You were right. I'm too intense. I don't know how to keep my distance when I get emotionally involved. I'm a good actor or you'd know that seeing you and not saying anything has been hell for me."

Having gotten this much off his chest, he seemed to unbend a little. Rachel could even sense a certain amusement in his eyes. "I'd take your advice and see a psychiatrist, Rachel, but I figure I wouldn't be much of a writer if he cured me."

"I think I worked that out for myself," Rachel answered. "Is that why you live up here? Because you become emotionally involved with everyone and everything?"

"I'm not that neurotic." He was smiling at her questions. "In the first place, living here gives me a degree of privacy I wouldn't have elsewhere. And it also allows me to control whom I see and when I see them. In spite of my mother's contention that I'm a hermit, that comes to a lot of interruptions. If I became emotionally involved with even half of the female ones I'd be so exhausted from the love affairs that there'd be no energy left for serious work."

The joke relaxed Rachel to the point of being able to say what she should have said initially. "I came upstairs to tell you how I feel, Jason. You were right when you said I need to know you better. In my own way I've been just as obsessed with you as you've been with me. I told you this afternoon that I'd hated you for a year and you called me on it. You knew I was ambivalent, but I only told you part of the reason why. The fact is, you understand me—the way I used to be—better than anyone, even my family, and there's a part of me that's always wanted your approval. As if—if Jason Wilder says I've changed, then I really must have."

He didn't seem surprised by her confession. "Of course you've changed. I told you that this afternoon."

"But am I attracted to you just because you wrote *Tragedy*, or because . . ."

"Suppose I was fat, bald and sixty-five. Would you still want to sleep with me?" he asked, apparently finding her tortured self-analysis funny.

"Laugh if you want to, but I'm never going to find out how I feel if I run away. I'm only afraid of hurting you if things don't work out the way you want them to."

"Ah! You're saying that you want to forget me then," he observed. "Get me out of your system."

"It might happen that way. And it seems to me that having an affair now, before we resolve our feelings, would be a mistake. Things are complicated enough already."

Her response seemed to annoy him. "What exactly do you want from me, Rachel? Sainthood? You know how much I want you. What am I supposed to do about the fact that you're sleeping in my house? Ignore it?"

"Control yourself!" Rachel snapped back, then immediately regretted losing her temper. "You're rushing me, Jason. I want to be sure I'm doing the right thing. I'm not exactly a swinger and this whole situation—it confuses me. It's like there are four people involved—you, me, Maria, and the author of *Tragedy*."

"I understand that. Just tell me one thing, Rachel. How much of your reluctance has to do with all the things you've mentioned and how much of it comes from a hang-up about sex? I mean, sleeping with Garcia wasn't exactly the high point of your day, am I right?"

Rachel, her face flushed, nodded. "I told you, you were right about everything."

Jason was silent for several long moments, a brooding look on his face. Finally he said to Rachel, "It's almost empathic, the instinct I had about you. When I was writing the bedroom scenes with you and Garcia I used to torture myself with the idea that the two of you—that he did the same things with you as he did with his mistress. I didn't want to picture you that way. It seemed all wrong."

"I never understood his attitude until I read your book," Rachel answered. "Was it all true? The things you wrote?"

"Sure. His mistress was angry about being left out of the will, so she spilled her guts to me. Someday

I'll show you the stuff I left out." He got up, walked around the coffee table and sat down next to Rachel.

When he slipped one hand around her back and tipped her chin up with his other hand she stiffened and tried to pull away. "Jason, please," she murmured. "This isn't going to accomplish . . ."

The words were cut off by his lips gently touching hers, making no demands on her. It was as if he was saying, "All right. We'll do things your way." She slowly relaxed, so that when he lifted his head and slid his arm around her shoulders it felt natural to nestle her head into the crook of his neck.

"Just remember that, from my point of view, I'm in love with you," he said softly. "You can call it obsessive, or neurotic, or any other damn thing you want, but that's how it *feels* to me. And as little as I like rejection, it's much better than having you take off for New York without giving me a chance. I won't rush you."

"I know you won't." Rachel turned her head, wanting him to see the gratitude in her eyes. Their lips, only inches apart, were somehow suddenly clinging. Jason's mouth, at first gentle and tender, gradually hardened, then teased, aroused, demanded. And Rachel, heat suffusing her body, started to lose control of her reactions. She closed her eyes and savored her own excitement, one hand going to Jason's waist, the other sliding up his neck to twine itself through his hair. The way he kissed her, the lazy, sensuous movements of his tongue, first exploring, then dominating, meshed with all her fantasies.

For a few minutes the hotly erotic kissing was enough. But there came a point when Rachel sensed Jason's frustration. His mouth was rougher and the hand he had slipped underneath her shirt tired of playing with her hardened nipples and started to caress her breasts possessively. She knew she wouldn't stop him. It was too intoxicating—this sensation of being out of control, of being subdued, malleable, eager to comply with Jason's wishes. She arched against his hand, allowed him to ravage her mouth, invited him to take whatever else he wanted.

When he pulled away she could only look at him in confusion. "That's enough for one night," he muttered. "I'm throwing you out."

"Why?" He still wanted her; it was obvious from the strained expression on his face.

"Because what you want physically and what you want in your mind are two different things, Rachel. The sex would be terrific—I'd make sure of it—but you'd feel lousy in the morning. Empty, resentful and manipulated."

He'd known that before she did, Rachel thought in wonderment. It was uncanny. Jason had moved away to the far end of the loveseat, his hands clasped in front of him, hanging between his knees. She caught the hint of a smile on his face and asked about the cause.

"You said control myself, so I'm controlling myself. I was smiling because it occurred to me that all those years as an actor weren't wasted." He was grinning crookedly by now. "Sometimes, especially in early rehearsals, before there was an audience or lights or cameras to distract me, I'd be doing a love scene and forget it was only a play or a movie. When I was single it wasn't any problem—co-stars go to bed together all the time. But afterwards, being faithful to Meredith took a lot of effort, especially given the attitudes of some of my leading ladies. It's a tribute to my self-control that they didn't have their way with me, Rachel."

Rachel was about to chastise him for his pomposity when he leaned over and kissed her nose. "I'm thirty-seven and you make me feel like a sex-starved high school freshman. Go downstairs and lock your door, lady."

As Rachel got up and walked toward the steps she could feel his eyes following her. She turned around to wish him good-night, but couldn't resist teasing instead. "On second thought, maybe I'll leave it open."

When he started to follow her she hurried down the stairs and into her room giggling.

Over the next two days nothing changed—and everything changed. Rachel's outward routine was exactly the same: riding and shopping in the morning, preparing the meals, writing, rowing and sunbathing in the afternoon. She wrote another letter to Susan, mailed the same day as the one written at the lake, telling her sister about what had just happened between Jason and herself and issuing an invitation to visit New Hampshire. But now she wanted something more from Susan than a mutual exchange of confidences. She wanted her sister to meet Jason and approve of him.

What had changed was the atmosphere in the house. Jason appeared to accept the status quo. As for Lady Bennett, she made no attempt to hide her pleasure with the increasing closeness between Jason and Rachel; she apparently considered herself a female Cupid, conveniently overlooking her original motive for asking Rachel up to New Hampshire.

Having made up her mind that her elder son was finally going to remarry, she facilitated the courtship by making herself as unobtrusive as possible.

Now, when Rachel brought Jason his breakfast or lunch, he smiled at her with a warmth that made her reservations seem unreasonable. After a Wednesday afternoon session at the hockey table almost exploded out of control they abandoned the penny arcade. Jason had eased up on Rachel, letting her take more shots, only to provoke a frigid accusation that he was patronizing her. Her anger had sparked his temper, which in turn had sparked his libido. It was obvious to both of them that they couldn't compete without winding up in the adjacent bedroom. So they no longer spent time with each other except in the evenings.

Each night after dinner they would go into the living room and talk for hours. Rachel told Jason all about the last four years: the daily routine of her life, the emotional changes she had undergone. Unconsciously, she related to him like a friend from the past—someone she had once been close to who had since drifted out of her life. She was merely bringing him up to date.

Rachel was the product of a traditional American family and yet, because of the Third World cultures she had grown up in, she had assimilated a conflicting mixture of values, some of which she ultimately rejected. Her girlhood view of the role of women, a very Latin one, had given way to a strong independent streak. Perhaps it had merely lain dormant inside her for years; her father, having no sons, had always encouraged his daughters to excel.

Since meeting Jason Wilder, however, a new

desire had started to grow in her; she wanted a loving, supportive relationship, someone to share her life with. This unexpected feeling told her just how much Jason was coming to mean to her. As a result, the doubts she felt often angered her, but they wouldn't disappear.

When she and Jason talked about marriage she said she didn't see it as incompatible with dual careers provided both partners agreed on what would come first: job or spouse. Jason, having been married to an ambitious actress, contributed his own experience to the discussion.

"One of the problems with my marriage to Meredith was that both of us put our careers first," he told her. "That might work for some people, but I learned that I wasn't happy with it. To me, the idea of partial commitment is inherently contradictory. I need to come first in a woman's life."

"I wish I could give you that," Rachel answered, "but I can't. There's so much between us that bothers me."

"Right." Rachel picked up the weariness in Jason's voice. "That's what this is all about. I'm trying to give you some time to work things out."

Along with time, Jason offered openness. For a man who guarded his privacy so zealously, he was unusually talkative about his past. Rachel was particularly interested in his childhood, in his feelings about the very dissimilar men his mother had married, Julian Wilder and Ronald Bennett.

"I used to wonder what would have happened to me if my father had lived," Jason told Rachel Thursday night. "His word was law around our house. My mother went along with it, probably because he was so much older than she was. He was as much a father figure as a lover to her. But if he hadn't died I think they would have divorced eventually. She would have started to assert herself and he wouldn't have been able to accept it. He was too rigid to change."

"And how did that affect you?" Rachel asked.

"The usual ways. My father had a definition of success which no one was supposed to question. He expected me to be the all-American kid—straight *A*s, a Little League star, the whole bit. He started talking about Harvard Law School before I finished kindergarten. Even though I was only ten when he died I can remember having the family history beaten into me." He gestured toward a Chippendale side table. "You see the furniture in this room? I could give you a two-hour lecture on it. I was a rebellious kid, but it never extended to the antiques. I love them."

"It was the first thing about you that attracted me." Smiling, Rachel corrected, "Well, *one* of the first things. I couldn't believe that a man with such impeccable taste could be the skunk I thought he was."

"That's something I have to thank him for, then. The only other favor he ever did for me was to die when he did."

Rachel's reaction to his bluntness showed in her face. She couldn't pretend to be shocked, but she was taken aback by the intensity of his dislike.

"I'm being honest, Rachel," he continued. "My father was overbearing and self-righteous. Fortunately, he was also a workaholic, which meant that a lot of the time he would give me an order, assume I'd obey it and then forget about it. My mother was supposed to follow up on it. She never questioned his authority when it came to *her*, but I was a different story. She was loving and protective and if she hadn't been around to run interference between me and my father he would have taken a belt to my backside much more often than he did. So we'd play the same game over and over. My father would tell me to do something—like enter a science fair that bored me to death—and I'd refuse. Since he was bigger and stronger than I was I usually ended up backing down. I was afraid of him. In the end my mother would do three-quarters of the project to satisfy him, just like I knew she would. It was a destructive, dishonest way to live and the situation could never have continued. By the time I hit adolescence I would have been his physical equal. And if he'd tried to beat me up I would have fought back."

Now Rachel *was* shocked. "Did he hit your mother?" she asked, sickened by the idea of what Jason had endured as a child.

"As far as I know, never. He doted on her, which might explain why he resented me. It's no accident that I was their only child. He didn't like the competition."

"And your stepfather? Was he different?"

"He was the best thing that ever happened to either of us. He's five years younger than my mother —twenty-eight when they got married. What makes Ronald special is not that he's smart—lots of people are smart. He's something even rarer, a genuinely open-minded person. He's made discoveries because he's willing to look at evidence that everyone else dismissed. When he met my mother I'd had her to myself for almost two years. A stepfather was the last thing I wanted. But Ronald tried to communicate with me, to understand me—and I responded to it. He's been as much a father to me as to my half-brother and half-sister, with the same open-mindedness he shows in his work. Given his social background he ordinarily would have sent me to one of the best public schools in England and I would have hated it. Instead, he found a small, unconventional school that gave me the freedom to do what I wanted. I understood that, in exchange, I would have to study some of what *they* wanted. My mother never approved of my interest in acting—she assumed I'd become a lawyer, like a dozen other Wilders. Ronald was the one who convinced her that it wasn't the end of the world."

In view of Lady Bennett's campaign to coax her son back onto the stage her initial disapproval came as a surprise. "She's certainly changed her mind, hasn't she? She's got a regular army coming up here tomorrow and all of them agree with her that you should do Stephen's play. It's been years since you acted in anything, Jason. Why don't you give it another try?"

"Because I'd rather spend my time writing, Rachel. I'm not going to take the lead in Stephen's play because a bunch of people think it would be psychologically beneficial for me."

"And that's the only reason?"

"It's enough of one," Jason answered curtly. "Don't start in on me about it."

After that, the subject was taboo. Rachel attributed Jason's uncharacteristic touchiness to mixed feelings. As much as he loved performing, he was disillusioned by the public's failure to accept him as anyone other than the dashing Hamlin Stone. And unlike most actors, he disliked publicity and was uncomfortable with being a celebrity.

But nearly five years had passed since his last film had been released. Other idols had taken his place. On a stage, freed from the tyranny of movie close-ups, he would be able to create any character he wished to. Even his appearance had changed—his face was less boyish now, tougher-looking.

Fundamentally, Rachel supposed, she just didn't understand how Jason could enjoy spending the bulk of his time sitting in an office, pounding away at a typewriter. As much as *she* enjoyed writing it was too sedentary, too solitary; she could never do it full time.

It was midnight; Rachel stifled a yawn and got up, admitting that she was about to fall asleep on the couch. Jason walked her up the stairs, his arm around her waist, and said good-night to her in front of her bedroom door. He kissed her passionately, just as he had the night before, his hand moving from her back to her breast, his mouth hungry yet controlled. And like the night before, he was the one who pulled away, leaving Rachel frustrated and disappointed.

Weariness loosened her tongue. "You do it to tease me, don't you?" she accused. "To punish me."

"Are you serious?" Judging by his tone, he thought she was either incredibly dense or plain mad. "I do it because I can't keep my hands off you and I pay the price every damn night. Just say the word and I'll carry you upstairs."

For all Rachel's physical longing she still had the

same mental reservations as forty-eight hours before. At most she was willing to let Jason take the initiative, to try to seduce her into his bed. She stared up at him for a few seconds, issuing a silent invitation, but he merely frowned moodily and walked away.

# Chapter Eight

The "New York Artillery," as Rachel had labeled the Pollocks and the Chapins, invaded New Hampshire shortly before dinner on Friday. As always, she was in and out of the dining room throughout the meal, a state of affairs which sometimes made it difficult for her to keep track of the conversation. On this occasion, however, the conversation skipped from subject to subject so unpredictably that it scarcely mattered when she left or reentered. Typical New Yorkers, each of them interjected opinions into the middle of someone else's sentences, shifted topics capriciously and seemed to think nothing of the fact that two or even more of them were frequently talking at once. Laughter and wit were the order of the evening.

Rachel was silent at first, taking stock of the participants. She recalled that Stephen Chapin was in his late thirties, although he looked somewhat younger. Tall, shaggy-haired and seemingly under-nourished, he delivered his thoughts in staccato bursts capable of baffling even a fellow New York intellectual. He had a habit of using his horn-rimmed glasses for emphasis, waving them in the air when he was excited about something or peering over the top of the frames when he wanted to challenge someone else's opinion. He invariably said exactly what he thought, seemingly unconcerned that his bluntness might be perceived as offensive or even insulting.

By comparison, Paula Chapin was positively laid-back. Although animated and attractive, she was less beautiful than her sister, Jacqueline Pollock. Her manner, however, was far warmer. Her comments revealed a pragmatism that balanced Stephen's abstruseness, exemplified by her acute retort to his rhapsody about a play they had recently seen together.

After ten minutes of hearing how poetic the author's use of language had been, how innovative his structure, Paula had arched an eyebrow at Stephen and drawled, "Unfortunately, darling, the only person in all of New York who understood it was you."

In the company of her equals, Jackie Pollock seemed far less overbearing than Rachel remembered. And she liked Jackie's husband Harry immediately. The fact that he so obviously appreciated her cooking would have won her over, even if his slightly gruff, unpretentious manner had not.

Enjoying a meal with these people, Rachel felt more stimulated and alive than at any time since leaving New York. Jason challenged her intelligence and aroused her body, but she missed the frenetic pace of an evening like this one. In short, she realized, she missed the pace of her life in the city.

By the middle of the meal she had started to contribute to the conversation, sometimes adding a wry perspective far different from that of the high-powered cultural insiders.

It was not until after dinner that the "New York Artillery" went to war against an outflanked Jason Wilder. Paula had helped Rachel clean up the kitchen; afterward the two of them walked into the parlor to see Stephen bounding down the steps, his arms laden with manuscripts. He stalked into the living room and handed them out, ignoring the dour look on Jason's face.

Jason motioned Rachel to sit down next to him, an invitation which surprised her, given his impersonality during dinner. She was even more surprised when he draped an arm around her shoulder and murmured into her ear, "I missed you when you were in the kitchen. Tomorrow . . ."

"Tomorrow *you* can help me clean up," she drawled, smiling at him.

"Tomorrow we'll go out," he corrected. He glanced at Stephen Chapin, apparently oblivious to the interest his husky tone and possessive air had created. "Okay, let's get this over with."

"I'm insulted," the playwright answered. "We're reading a work of genius here, Wilder, not some superficial musical comedy." He imbued the last phrase with crushing disdain.

Jason turned to the first page of the manuscript, glanced at the cast of characters and delivered the first line. His part was that of a congressman who had served just long enough to experience his first taste of political power. The other major characters were his chief of staff, his married mistress and her Cabinet-member husband.

As the reading progressed, Jason became increasingly absorbed in his role, forgetting that Rachel was even next to him. He clutched the script with both hands and read his lines with such convincing passion that it was difficult to believe that the play was entirely new to him. It didn't seem to matter that no one else could approach the intensity of his performance—he was completely caught up in his character.

Harry Pollock, Jason and the Chapins were reading the play aloud; the other three people in the room provided an audience. Rachel found that her imagination filled in the missing visual element. The themes of the play were timeless: altruism versus temptation, the abuse of power, selflessness and self-deception. Although the characters could hardly be called ordinary people, Chapin brought them to life, made their actions plausible, induced the audience to care about what happened to them. When the reading ended Jackie Pollock, Rachel and Lady Bennett spontaneously applauded. Jason leaned back on the couch with the exhausted but satisfied look of a man who's spent the entire night making love.

"We know how you feel about the time frame here, so we're not going to ask for out-of-town reviews," Harry Pollock said to Jason. "I booked the theater for early February. I'm willing to go with a three-month contract with a provision . . ."

Jason interrupted him. "Find yourself another congressman. The play's damn good, but I'm not going to do it."

"That's a hell of a spot to leave us in," Stephen said. "It's a little late . . ."

"It's not my problem! I'm writing a novel, remember?"

"Talk to him, dear. Make him see reason." To Rachel's astonishment Jackie Pollock's heartrending plea was directed at *her*.

She had no intention of throwing herself into the fray. She had learned from more than one source that Jason Wilder hated to be nagged about anything and, after last night, knew that the subject of acting was one to be avoided. Besides, it was impossible to believe that some other actor hadn't already been lined up for the lead given Jason's previous refusals.

"Speaking as a theater fan, I'd like to see you do the play," she said to Jason. His reaction was immediate. By all rights, the cold anger in his eyes should have frozen her to the couch. "But on the other hand," she quickly added, "speaking as a reader, I'd like to see you finish the novel."

Her qualification failed to mollify him. "Spoken like a true diplomat's daughter," he drawled.

Rachel was already annoyed with Jason for unleashing his anger at her, she only wanted to stay out of this, and his sarcasm provoked her into speaking her mind. Besides, her background was a topic *she* preferred to avoid, and she knew that the surest way to accomplish that was by refocussing the conversation on Jason.

"All right, then, I'll tell you what I think," she said to him. "I wonder how much longer you're going to bury yourself up here, Jason. You love to act—even a cretin could have seen that tonight. But you're afraid, aren't you? You think the audience will come expecting Hamlin Stone. Well, maybe they will, but it's how they *leave* that counts. Where's your faith in yourself? Where are your guts?"

Jason's face was taut with fury, making Rachel regret her burst of temper. "Quite the little psychoanalyst, aren't you?" he said. "Nothing like experience, sweetheart."

Rachel's inward flinch was well-hidden. No matter how enraged Jason was, hitting below the belt that way was unjustifiable. Her self-control evaporated. No man treated her that way and escaped unscathed.

She smiled at Stephen Chapin, who seemed to be enjoying the fireworks blazing around him, and said, "You know the *real* reason why he's refusing, don't you, Stephen?"

He shook his head, smiling back at her.

"Jason just isn't comfortable with the role." Rachel's voice was syrupy enough to pour. "You need to add a few scenes so he'll feel at home. First of all, he keeps his clothes on throughout the entire play, and second, all of the other characters are human. Couldn't you fix it up?"

Paula Chapin was the first to laugh, followed by everyone but Jason. His whole body was rigid, a stony look in his eyes. "Where's your sense of humor?" Stephen needled. "It *was* funny."

"I agree," Jason answered stiffly. "But I'll remind you that you're my guest up here, Stephen." He turned to Rachel, glaring at her. "And as for *you, you're* my employee. I don't enjoy having the bunch of you pounding away at me, and if you're going to spend the whole weekend at it you can find a hotel to stay in." Having made his position crystal clear he stalked out of the room, slamming the door behind him.

Rachel hesitated only a moment before running

after him. When she caught up to him at the top of the steps she grabbed at his arm and hissed, "Who do you think you are, with that '*you're* my employee' business? You don't *own* me, Jason. I'll say what I think just like everyone else around here."

"That wasn't why you started in on me. *I* said 'diplomat's daughter' and *you* panicked and changed the subject. Why are you so defensive about it?"

"Why are you so defensive about acting again? The fact is, it makes me uncomfortable. That's all you need to know."

"Right. And don't you think it makes *me* uncomfortable to have to sit there and listen to your sanctimonious analysis of my emotions? I know how I feel, Rachel. I don't need you or anyone else to tell me. I'm not defensive. But I'm not going to be badgered."

Rachel was forced to admit that much of what he said was true. Even so, he had gone too far and she wasn't letting him get away without an apology. "I'm sorry if I sounded sanctimonious," she began, wanting to be fair. "But that crack about my therapy was nasty, Jason. And calling me your employee . . . everyone can see there's something between us. It made me feel like your paid mistress."

"You're oversensitive. I meant that you *act* like a psychoanalyst, Rachel. You pick apart motivations instead of listening to emotions." Jason's voice was gentler now, his anger aparently waning. "The other comment was a cheap shot, but I'm sure no one else interpreted it the way you did. I don't want to be your boss, or pay for your body." He smiled at her, trailed a teasing finger down her cheek, and added softly, "I admit that I've fantasized about being your master, though."

Rachel's emotions, already heightened by their argument, flared with arousal at his teasing words and provocative look. She was still clutching his arm, but loosened her grip and slowly returned his smile. "And when you had that fantasy, what did you order your slave to do?" she purred.

In reply, he bent his head and kissed her, a tantalizing assault on her defenses intended to frustrate rather than satisfy. His lips stroked persuasively, his tongue not quite invading her mouth. Rachel slid her arms around his neck and arched against him, aching to have him deepen the kiss. Her tongue slid past his to explore his mouth, seeking to undermine the control he was so obviously exerting over himself. At first she thought she'd succeeded—Jason responded with a rough passion, kissing her almost savagely, holding her hips and moving against her with a seductive demand. Then he pulled away and growled, "Do you want me to make love to you?"

Rachel could think about nothing else. "Yes," she whispered.

Jason straightened and Rachel watched uneasily as a smug expression came over his features. "Good. That means that by tomorrow night you'll be begging me for it."

Rachel could scarcely believe what she was hearing. Jason had his dark side, but vengeful nastiness wasn't a normal part of it. Becoming angry, she asked herself what kind of game he thought he was playing to lead her on and then reject her. "You're a bastard," she said softly.

He simply smiled. "So you finally figured out that I'm human. I admit I'm punishing you, Rachel. It feels very good, after the hell you've put me through for the last few nights. But even more than that, I'm tired and I'm in a lousy mood and I'm still angry with you. I've also decided that there are a few things you need to work out before I take you to bed."

The arrogance of that comment enraged her. "Don't do me any favors!" she snapped.

"But I will. Tomorrow night," he replied. "And I guarantee you're going to love it."

Even the knowledge that Jason was for some reason deliberately baiting her couldn't calm Rachel's fury. When he turned his back to her, she yelled at him, "You're pompous and egotistical and I hate you!"

He half-turned, looking back over his shoulder. "If I crooked my finger," he drawled, "you'd come with me."

Rachel's mood was no less antagonistic by the following morning. She couldn't ride since Lady Bennett and her guests had commandeered all the horses so she took Synge for a long walk and returned to find everyone eating breakfast. Even Jason, in a departure from his usual routine, was sitting at the dining room table chatting quite amiably with Stephen and Paula.

They exchanged a look—Jason amused, Rachel hostile—which Lady Bennett coolly intercepted. "We're going off for the day, Rachel," she said. "There's an art show in Hanover we're going to visit, and of course we'll stop in on the Foxworths while we're there. Will you join us?"

Given Rachel's mood she couldn't face the prospect of touring the countryside with these people. But being alone in the same house with Jason was even less palatable. Judging by his smile, he clearly understood her dilemma.

"I'm going along," he said.

"Then I'll stay home," Rachel answered.

The fact that he laughed at her petulance only angered her further. "We'll be back in time for dinner. I'm giving you the night off tonight—we're going out. Do you own anything besides jeans?"

Everyone was watching Rachel, waiting for her to explode. She realized that she was only providing entertainment for all of them, acting like a balky child. She had a weapon much more effective than sarcasm at her disposal.

"I brought up a jumpsuit, Jason," she said, taunting him with the self-contained, distancing tone that she used to frustrate him with during their hockey games. She turned to Lady Bennett, smiling. "It's made of a silky fabric, Olivia, kind of clingy and feminine. Is that okay?"

It was Jason who answered her question. "I'll look forward to it," he drawled.

Rachel went into the kitchen to fix herself breakfast, so resentful that she all but threw the bread into the toaster. It wasn't enough to punish Jason with coolness, she was going to put him through agony for his rejection of her last night and for amusing himself at her expense this morning. She silently promised herself that tonight's dinner was going to be the longest of his life. He thought he could snap his fingers and bring her to heel, did he? Tonight he would find out what provocation really meant. He would also have the door slammed in his face at the most painful moment possible.

She didn't hear him come into the kitchen. She was buttering her toast and almost dropped the knife when she felt his hands come down on her shoulders.

"I love you," he said, nibbling at her ear.

Rachel's body was rigid with anger. "You have a funny way of showing it."

He slid his hands to her waist, caressing her unresponsive body. "I was a rat. I admit it. But I suffered more than you did. It was the worst night I've spent since you got here."

"Good!" Rachel snapped.

He backed away from her, saying rather mournfully that he could see she wasn't ready to forgive him, and left. Fortunately, he had also left the dining room by the time she carried in her breakfast so she was able to relax and join in the conversation.

She worked in the kitchen for the first half-hour after everyone left, cleaning counters that didn't need it and mopping an already spotless floor. Physical activity didn't keep her from brooding about her feelings toward Jason, silently enumerating both his good and bad points.

She couldn't stay angry with a man who touched her so sensuously and who said "I love you" with such sincerity. It was just that she had seen a side of him last night that she hadn't known existed and hadn't been prepared for. She supposed that a combination of factors had been at play: physical frustration, anger over being the topic of conversation, a feeling that the woman he loved should understand and support his point of view, at least when others were present.

Eventually Rachel realized that she was mentally writing the biographical profile she had initially come to New Hampshire to do. If she didn't put the words down on paper she would never get them out of her system.

She settled herself into Jason's office and began to write, finding that the words came much more easily than usual. "Karen Rideau is Jason Wilder's house-keeper," she typed. "A maternal, hardworking woman of twenty-four, she has seen many facets of the complex man she works for. Once, she admits, she made the mistake of repeatedly nagging him to eat lunch, unthinkingly addressing him in the same tone of voice she uses with her little sons. The proffered tunafish sandwich was thrown across the room onto the floor, Karen's stammered apology interrupted with a torrent of blue language.

"Paul Rideau is Karen's husband. A cabinetmaker and carpenter, he helped in the restoration of Wilder's Georgian home in the New Hampshire woods. Last year Paul was in an accident that burned his face and upper body, almost depriving him of the use of his eyes and hands. Wilder arranged for expert medical care, flew Paul to Boston in his private plane and insisted on paying most of the bills. Karen's comments about her famous boss: 'I can't say enough about him. He's the kindest man in the world. But,' she adds with a smile, 'I've learned to stay away from him when he's grouchy.'"

Rachel went on to fully develop the theme of Jason Wilder's complexity. She left out nothing, including even the deeply personal remarks he had made about his childhood and marriage and his conflicting feelings about his career as an actor. By the time she finished a second draft her anger was long forgotten. So much in Jason was admirable: his capacity for love, his sensitivity, his concern for others. Rachel suspected that even his dangerous, unpredictable side attracted her; she was a person who needed excitement in her life and Jason could certainly provide it.

She no longer questioned her love for him, although she would never have claimed that her feelings were the result of any positive qualities he might have. Love was an irrational emotion and might as easily stem from his authorship of *A Latin American Tragedy* as from anything else. But the whys and hows no longer mattered to her. Like Jason, she only knew that she felt herself to be in love. He might accuse her of overanalyzing her emotions, but in fact, such a task was totally beyond her at present.

If a dollop of resentment remained over her treatment at Jason's hands the night before, the prospect of revenge was so sweetly entrancing that Rachel's primary emotion was a mischievous delight at what she intended to put him through. In her fantasies, he was racked by frustrated passion by the time they finally arrived home. She pictured him aching to touch her, begging her to let him make love to her, and her own mocking refusal. What she really wanted was for him to override her objections, not painfully, but just forcefully enough to make the whole experience unbearably exciting.

She dressed to look sensuous, something she hadn't bothered with in years. Her hair was gathered into a loose knot on top of her head, stray tendrils hanging out, inviting a man's caress. The jumpsuit she wore was not revealing in the sense of exposing a great deal of bare skin; on the contrary, the long sleeves, mandarin collar and zippered front merely hinted at what lay hidden. But the silver-shot blue fabric shimmered when she walked and clung when she didn't, and would have aroused even a snow-man.

Rachel had a weakness for sexy lingerie and had put on her favorite white teddy underneath the jumpsuit. It was an expensive French import her sister had given her as a birthday present. The one-piece garment, all open-work lace and body-hugging silk, had tiny mother-of-pearl buttons down the front, which she pictured Jason unfastening. She felt irresistible the moment she put it on.

Jason was waiting in the parlor when Rachel came down the stairs and he reacted just as she had wanted him to, his gaze raking her body, his eyes both accusing and amused. "I hope that's for my benefit," he said.

Rachel slipped an arm through one of his. He had changed into a navy blazer and charcoal slacks and looked so handsome that he belonged on a movie screen. Which was, unfortunately, exactly where he refused to be.

"Of course it's for your benefit," she answered. "I've spent the whole day missing you . . . and wanting you."

"And now I'm going to pay for it, hmm?"

Rachel smiled but said nothing. They took two cars to the restaurant, Lady Bennett with the Pollocks in their Cadillac, and Jason, Rachel and the Chapins in Jason's Oldsmobile. Rachel sat close to Jason on the front seat, her leg touching his, her hand restless against his thigh. She was well aware that he had to struggle to keep his mind on the conversation, and reveled in it.

They pulled into a space in the restaurant parking lot; Jason switched off the engine but made no move to get out of the car. "Go ahead," he said to Stephen and Paula. "We'll be in in a minute."

As soon as the Chapins slammed the back door, Rachel asked innocently, "Is something the matter?"

"Are you going to keep this up all night?" Jason demanded.

"Keep what up?"

"You know what I'd like to do to you, Rachel?"

"In the car?" she teased.

Her punishment was a rough, searing kiss which Rachel refused to respond to. Jason slowly pulled away, looking even angrier than before, and was about to speak when Rachel put a finger over his lips.

"Like this," she whispered. Her lips grazed his mouth provocatively, then flitted away. Jason caught at her chin and forced her mouth back up to his own, kissing her with the same leashed passion he had demonstrated at their first embrace.

Several minutes passed before he buried his face against her neck. "We have to go inside," he murmured, "but later . . ."

"Later, you can kiss me good-night at my door."

He straightened, took in her smile. "Right," he said. "Tomorrow morning."

They walked arm-in-arm into the restaurant, a large, Colonial-style house which had been renovated for dining. Lady Bennett's friends, Nancy and Jack Foxworth, were joining them for dinner, and the party of nine was soon seated at a large circular table in one of the private dining rooms.

Like the night before, the conversation was eclectic, skipping from horses to the courses Jack Foxworth taught at Dartmouth to Nancy's sculpture exhibit to Sir Ronald's expedition. All mention of the theater was tactfully avoided. Rachel, even more animated than usual due to thoughts of what lay ahead, contributed a favorite anecdote about a luncheon buffet as full of slapstick as a silent comedy. Host and hostess were an estranged couple who were giving the party in the honor of their newly-engaged daughter. They had skirted disaster for three solid hours, but when the guests finally left ex-husband and wife exploded. They wound up in a fight, the leftovers got thrown all over the patio and Susan and Rachel fled without being paid. The check arrived by messenger the following day.

While Rachel was talking she inched her chair closer to Jason's, slipped off her shoe and ran her toes along his calf. He wasn't, she noticed, laughing quite as hard as the others.

When she finished the story Nancy Foxworth asked her how she had gotten into the catering business. Rachel explained that the idea was originally her sister's and that Susan had trained to be a chef. "We also do desserts for a local restaurant," she added. "Susan teaches a few courses a year and I do free-lance articles for women's and gourmet magazines. Being busy keeps me out of trouble."

"Looking at her now you'd never guess that she was the premier social butterfly of her generation, would you?" Jason remarked.

Rachel felt herself pale. She might have been teasing him tonight but he knew it was only a game that she had every intention of finishing. Nothing she had done merited such cutting retaliation. He knew how she felt about the subject of her past.

She started to tremble when Stephen Chapin asked for further information. Jason blithely informed him that Rachel was the inspiration for his second book. "Her married name was Raquel Garcia Martinez. She was the model for Maria."

Even though Rachel was staring at her plate she could feel everyone looking at her. And then Jason went on, "I once told Rachel that I fell in love with Maria's potential and hated her for wasting it. I met Rachel and never stood a chance. I was captivated within minutes and in love in less than a week."

Whatever his motive for these revelations, it wasn't a desire for revenge, Rachel realized. His declaration of love had been delivered with a quiet intensity that left no one in doubt of his feelings. As for everyone's reactions, Rachel sensed astonishment and fascination, but certainly not the disdain she had always dreaded.

Stephen Chapin started to question her, probing her emotions and motives. Uncomfortable with the catechism, Rachel finally told him, "It's all in Jason's book. If you want to know what I was like, just reread it."

"But afterward," Stephen persisted. "When you came back to New York, what motivated you to . . ."

"Rachel's had enough of being a media heroine," Jason interrupted. "If you're thinking of using her in a play, Stephen, don't."

His tone was firm, protective. Stephen denied any such intentions and resumed his questioning. Rachel was honest, but only to a point. She admitted to pain, but glossed over the depth of it. In talking of her life now, she told Stephen, "In Latin America I had no confidence in my ability to succeed at anything that didn't depend on my looks or my position. For a long time afterward I felt like everything might fall apart. But I think I've finally accepted the fact that I'm a capable person."

"How could you have thought you weren't?" Jason asked, his eyes warm and teasing. "I'll bet you were the best shopper in Santandia. Gave the best parties. No one knew how to put on make-up like you did, Rachel. Your efforts were just misdirected. If you had put the same energy into politics that you put into visiting people . . ."

"One more word out of you and I'll pour wine over your head," Rachel interrupted. She was smiling, just as the others were. Now she understood why Jason had re-introduced the subject of her past. Last night her insecurity had disturbed him, even angered him. He wanted her to see that her fears were baseless, that anyone worth knowing would admire her for her accomplishments not condemn her for past failings. He had shown her that she could look back on painful times and manage to laugh at them and she was grateful for that.

For several days now it had bothered Rachel that Jason didn't know her initial reason for coming to New Hampshire. She hadn't brought it up because she was afraid of his reaction. It seemed foolish to risk a fight over an idea she had quickly abandoned. But now, certain that he loved her too much to be seriously angry with her, she wanted to confess.

"I was very depressed when the book came out," she said to Stephen, "and very angry with Jason for invading my privacy. I wanted to get back at him. So when Olivia invited me up here I decided I'd write a biographical profile of him. I knew he'd hate it and I wanted him to know how I had felt." She glanced at Jason to see how he was taking this piece of news. He was obviously less than pleased, but didn't look particularly angry.

Rachel knew she was being nasty, but couldn't resist provoking him. The idea of straightening it out later—in private—was much too irresistible. "I finished it this afternoon, while you were gone," she said to Jason. "It's only a draft, and it needs more work, but where do you think I should publish it when it's done?" He missed the wink she sent in Lady Bennett's direction.

"That's *your* decision," he said stiffly.

And then Lady Bennett, in one of her deliberately obfuscating monologues, started talking about a charity affair she had agreed to chair. Throughout the rest of the meal Jason became progressively more withdrawn. At first Rachel continued to tease him, unable to believe that he could have taken her seriously. But when there was no response to her wandering hands she became as subdued as he was and more than a little alarmed. He reminded her of a time bomb, methodically ticking away.

They were in the middle of coffee when Jason stood up and told everyone, "I'm taking Rachel back to the house."

Normally she would have refused to go. She hadn't finished dessert and no overbearing man was going to stop her from doing so. But in this case she decided to relax her principles. Jason seemed angry enough to pick her up and sling her over his shoulder if she resisted.

As soon as they were seated in the car she told him, "I'm not really going to publish it, Jason. I was only kidding you."

"Sure you were. Drop me a postcard when it comes out, Rachel. I wouldn't want to miss it."

"Will you listen to me? I told you, I'm not going to publish it. I wouldn't do that to you."

"Then why write it?" he asked.

"I was upset about last night. I wanted to get my feelings down on paper."

"Tell me another one. You've been hot for revenge ever since you came here. I can't stop you, but I can make you pay for the privilege."

Rachel gave up arguing. She had never seen Jason so irrational, but he would undoubtedly cool down during the trip home. Obviously she had underestimated the extent to which he valued his privacy.

Back at the house, as he followed her up the stairs, she could feel his hostility as strongly as ever. She went into her room and started to close the door, only to have Jason force it open. He stepped inside and kicked it shut behind both of them. "Give it to me, Rachel. I want to read it."

Rachel silently handed him the manuscript, waiting for him to tear it up. Instead, he read it carefully, seeming to settle down as he proceeded. Only when he was finished did Rachel understand that this apparent calmness was actually icy determination. She repeated her earlier promise. "I'm not going to publish it, Jason. You can burn it if you want to."

He ignored her completely, tossing the manuscript back onto the dresser. "It's a nice piece of work, but you left one thing out. Take off your clothes and we'll remedy that."

Rachel wasn't about to let him touch her—not in anger. "You can't come in here and tell me what to do," she said. "Please leave, Jason."

"You've had your hands on me all evening. That thing you're wearing—you knew what it would do to me. Take it off or I'll rip it off, Rachel."

He actually meant it. There was no one in the house to call on for help and no way to escape him. Rachel couldn't believe that he was capable of violence. He had controlled himself with Meredith Lloyd under far more provoking circumstances. "I'm not going to let you make love to me, Jason. Not until we talk this out. I know you're not going to force me. You're not that type of man."

Again, he paid absolutely no attention to her, coming up behind her, seizing her hands and pinning them behind her back. Rachel struggled, only to have him slip his free arm around her body just under her breasts, holding her motionless. Although her heart was thudding in fear she was determined to give no other sign of her feelings. At least he wasn't hurting her, she thought.

"Take off the jumpsuit, Rachel," he repeated.

She heard the command as if from a distance, as if the whole thing were happening to somebody else. Jason would never address her in such a harsh tone of voice or treat her with such contempt. He loved her, didn't he?

Dry-mouthed, she nodded, not knowing what else to do. Although he immediately released her he was still standing close behind her, ready to recapture her if she tried to leave.

For just a moment all the fight went out of Rachel. She unzipped the jumpsuit and slithered out of it, totally unaware that her movements were as sensuous as a striptease. Only when Jason picked her up and tossed her onto the bed did she regain the wit to resist. She started to get up, seeking an escape that didn't exist, only to find her body straddled by his, her hands pinned above her head.

"I won't hurt you, Rachel," he said, pushing aside a strap of her teddy and running his fingers along the top of her breast, "if you do what I tell you to." He pulled all the pins out of her hair, tossing them on the floor, and then stared at the tiny buttons on the front of her teddy. "Very sexy. Unbutton them for me."

One look at the coldness on his face told her that it was useless to argue or plead. She forced herself to stare back just as icily. "If you don't stop this I'll hate you forever," she said, her voice amazingly steady.

He ignored the threat. "I'm getting impatient, Rachel." Her right hand was released and guided down to the top button of the teddy.

Rachel couldn't keep her hand from shaking, so much so that she wouldn't have been able to undo the tiny buttons even if she had wanted to. She tried to pull away, twisting her body in vain, only to have the free hand pinned above her head once again. A moment later she was struggling frantically, her control destroyed.

"Hey! Hold it!" Jason said. "If you don't stop squirming around like that you're going to drive me so crazy that I really *will* lose control of myself."

His voice, so full of laughter, drew Rachel's eyes to his face. He was grinning at her in such a perfectly normal fashion that she went limp in relief.

"You teased me all night long," he went on, releasing her wrists. "You wanted to provoke me, make me want you like hell, and you even let me know that you planned to say no just so I'd refuse to accept it. I thought I was giving you the love scene you wanted, but it just hit me that you're totally in the dark. You really are scared of me."

"You—you were never really angry?" Rachel asked. "You were just—acting?"

"I'm gratified that you appreciate the caliber of my performance, but try to remember that it's *only* a performance." Jason said with a wink. "I'm not stupid, Rachel. Once I found out you were a writer it didn't take much time to figure out why you came up here. And I know you won't publish anything I don't want you to."

"Then why didn't you say anything? I was afraid to tell you about it."

"I wanted you to trust me enough to bring it up yourself, which you did, tonight. I was looking for something to start a fight about . . ."

". . . to set this up?" Rachel asked.

"Of course."

She started to giggle. "Being with you is an adventure, Jason Wilder."

"Okay, Rachel, move it! I'm not going to wait all year!" Jason had slipped back into character so quickly, his voice so abrasive and impatient, that Rachel visibly started. She had to remind herself that the whole performance was solely for her benefit.

She started to slowly unbutton the teddy—too slowly, as it turned out. Before she could stop him, Jason was barking, "I told you, don't keep me waiting!" and had ripped the teddy down to her navel.

Her annoyance flared. "Jason, my sister gave me this! You didn't have to . . ."

"Shut up!" And then his hands were on her body, caressing the curve of her waist, cupping her breasts, massaging her nipples just roughly enough to arouse her into forgetting about the torn garment. He waited until her eyes were heavy with desire, then demanded, "Undress me, Rachel."

She wanted nothing more, but knew he would be disappointed if she submitted too easily. "Take your hands off me!" she snapped, renewing her struggles.

He moved so gracefully and so rapidly that she never had time to guess his intention. One moment he was straddling her hip, the next she was pinned face down on his lap.

"You lay one hand on me, Jason Wilder, and I'll never forgive you," she threatened, meaning every word of it.

He laughed softly. "Like this, you mean?" His hand feathered up her thigh, then slipped under the teddy to explore the softness beneath. "Or this?" The caress became more intimate.

Heat rippled through Rachel's body, making her moan with excitement. Jason held her captive for endless agonizing minutes, teasing her with gentle caresses until she was breathless with desire. Then he pulled her up into his arms.

He played with her lips, brushing his mouth over her own, until she ached with impatience. When his tongue began to probe her mouth the kiss was so hotly dominating that Rachel might have objected had she been less aroused—or less in love.

She wondered if the display of mastery was part of the game and soon had her answer. Jason broke the kiss, held her away from him and repeated his earlier demand. "Undress me, Rachel." But this time it came out as a husky, impassioned plea, rather than as an order.

The operation was clumsy at best, both of them fumbling with Jason's clothes, which ended up in a heap on the floor, Rachel's torn teddy on top. More than once she had imagined how it would be the first time they made love together. There would be privacy and tenderness and the time to enjoy both. She would have the freedom to explore his body, to arouse him as wildly as he'd aroused her.

Reality was nothing like that. Reality was a searing kiss so emotional and impassioned that Rachel could only cling to him and return it. Reality was his possession, too urgent to be gentle, and her own response, not tender but animalistic, her nails digging into his back. Reality was her quick, hot reaction to his lovemaking. She was aroused far beyond the point of control long before she wanted to be. But if she was overpowered by Jason the opposite was equally true for him.

It was over much too quickly, the intensity of it leaving them weak in each other's arms. Rachel felt dizzy with satisfaction; even after they separated, the room only slowly stopped drifting. "Thank you," she murmured.

"I think I'm supposed to tell *you* that," he answered, smiling at her, inviting her to nestle into the crook of his arm. "That thing you were wearing under the jumpsuit—what do you call it?"

"A teddy," Rachel said. "It cost a fortune. It wasn't very nice of you to ruin it."

"That's true, but I enjoyed it. I've never ripped off a woman's clothing before. Not even in the movies. It gave me a real sense of power."

He was half-teasing, half-serious. "Don't you dare bully me, Jason Wilder," Rachel said. "Because if you do, I'll . . . I'll . . ." She groped for an appropriate threat.

"Hmmm?"

"I'll force-feed you tuna fish sandwiches with bottled mayonnaise," she said, dissolving into giggles.

He laughed along with her, promising to buy her a new teddy. Then their eyes caught and held, and the laughter stopped. "I love you very much, Rachel," Jason murmured. "I know you have doubts about your own feelings . . ."

"I know that I love you, Jason. I just don't know why," Rachel interrupted.

"Always the analyst," he mocked. "Why don't you just accept the way you feel instead of trying to dissect it?"

She could only answer that it was important to her to understand herself. "For so long I never thought about the way I was, or what I could become. I just reacted, like a spoiled little girl. I don't want to be that way anymore."

"Does it still bother you? The thing about Maria?"

"Of course it does. It also bothers me that I had a hang-up about you before I even met you. I tell myself that it shouldn't matter, but I'm worried about whether what we feel is real, whether it will last."

"So why did you decide to sleep with me if you still had doubts?"

"Because I love you. Only time will answer my questions." She snuggled closer to him, smiling a little. "Besides, you're so sexy that I couldn't resist you."

"Sexy enough to marry?"

Although they had talked about marriage in the abstract his proposal surprised her. She knew he loved her, knew he wanted to be with her, and yet his first attempt at marriage had been so deeply painful to him that she had unconsciously assumed he would take his time about trying again.

"I don't want to rush you," he said, misinterpreting her silence. "But when you think it over, remember that I love you. I want to share my life with you. I want us to have a family together."

Rachel had forgotten how much he wanted children. Since he had literally written the book on her, he of all people had to know that a family was out of the question. Puzzled, she asked him, "Adopt, you mean?"

"Why should we want to . . ." He stopped in mid-sentence, muttering, "You don't know. I'll be damned." Then he continued more clearly, "Either you've been lucky without knowing it, or . . . Am I your first lover since Garcia died?"

Rachel didn't understand what Jason was talking about. Surely his last question was unnecessary. "I couldn't let a man that close—emotionally *or* physically. You understand me so well, I thought you realized that."

"If I seemed to assume it's only because I wanted to think so. I've found out that I'm so possessive about you that I don't even like the idea of your first marriage. *Garcia* was the one who couldn't have children, Rachel. Those two 'sons' of his belonged to his twenty-six-year-old nephew, Luis. Garcia never knew it, but he and his nephew shared the same mistress. She very deliberately became pregnant by Luis and passed the kids off as Garcia's. She knew he'd never have legitimate children and believed her sons would become his heirs. The idea was ludicrous, given the society, but people's capacity for self-deception is endless. She was furious when she found out about the will. She expected to be set for life."

Although rationally Rachel knew that the inability to bear children did not make her less of a woman, psychologically she suddenly felt whole in a way that she hadn't before. She gave Jason a hug, as though rewarding him for some wonderful gift.

He smiled at her, reading her thoughts. "It's a

fairly bizarre way to find out. You realize I might have gotten you pregnant?" He sounded only too pleased by that idea. "In a way, I hope I did. You wouldn't give me such an argument about marriage."

Rachel did some quick arithmetic. "It's the wrong time of the month. Besides," she pointed out, "times have changed. A woman doesn't automatically get married just because she's pregnant."

He looked at her as though she'd just punched him in the stomach. It took Rachel only a moment to understand the assumption he was making. "Oh, no, Jason, I'd never do that. *Never.*"

"No." He paused, his eyes softening. "No, of course you wouldn't." He took a strand of her hair and wound it around his index finger. Rachel felt a flush of excitement warm her body. She twisted sideways to kiss him, one leg hooked over his thigh, the kiss beginning at the corners of his mouth before she nibbled her way along his lower lip.

"I should send you up to your room," she murmured. "You've already given me enough material for my article."

"Lady," he answered hoarsely, "I haven't even begun."

He taught her what lovemaking was all about. Now, with their initial urgency burnt out, they were able to take the time to explore, to arouse, to give each other pleasure. Though guided at first by Jason, Rachel soon took the initiative. Her lips and hands grazed his body, learning every contour and discovering a few slight imperfections in the process.

"You're finding out all my faults," he said, smiling at the way she was massaging his side.

"Other women . . ."

178

"Groupies—they wanted something different. It wasn't like this, Rachel. I didn't want it to be."

Rachel liked the idea that her knowledge of him was exclusive, that the millions of women who had seen him on the screen didn't share it and that the other women who had embraced him had been denied it. Ultimately he covered her hand to still its teasing and pulled her back into his arms, kissing her deep and hard. "Now it's *my* turn," he growled.

He was gentle and deliberate, slowly building her arousal. On a stage he might have similarly excited an audience, involving them gradually until the accelerating tension exploded in a torrent of emotion at the end of the performance. He worked the same magic on her body, his hands and mouth increasingly intimate, stopping only when she whispered, "Jason, please. No more."

His actual possession was equally controlled. When he pulled her on top of him, Rachel thought that they were in the last scene of a three-act play. What she discovered was that the play had five acts, with enough intermissions to provide the sweetest sort of frustration. Both of them were exhausted afterward, their passion deliciously sated. They were too tired to say more than "I love you" to each other and then cuddle up in each other's arms.

*Chapter Nine*

It had taken Rachel a long time to trust, to share, to risk taking love as well as giving it. Her marriage to Carlos had started to wither within their first twelve months together. During the following year she had lived from month to month, unable to make a decision about the future. Ever since, she had been so absorbed in the relentless task of self-transformation that the absence of a lover had left no perceptible void in her life.

It was early in the morning and she was lying in bed alone. Jason had left her sometime during the night, while she was asleep, but first he had gone outside to cut her a rose from the garden. He had put it into a bud vase and set it on her nighttable and she had awakened to the scent of its perfume.

Experience had taught Rachel to be realistic, even in the face of such a flagrantly romantic gesture. In a mythical sense she and Jason might have known each other for many years, but in reality they had met just two weeks before. Though their time together had been unusually intense one didn't plunge into marriage after a scant fifteen days. Even in the best of circumstances one tried to be realistic, and these were definitely not the best of circumstances.

Rachel was troubled not only by the psychological factors at play in her relationship with Jason, but also by their differing needs for outside diversion. In her more restless moments she had told herself that the isolation of Linwood could easily drive her into the even greater isolation of a padded cell. She needed people around her, museums and theaters and concerts. She needed the excitement which only a major city could provide.

She doubted that Jason fully understood her feelings. Although a sensitive, perceptive man, he was used to doing exactly as he pleased, just as Rachel was. And, like Rachel, he had come to expect that others would accomodate him. When he talked about marriage he was tacitly assuming that she would give up her career in New York in order to live with him in New Hampshire.

It was one thing to acknowledge these problems to herself and another to confront Jason with them. They still had almost three weeks together and, to Rachel, that seemed like a great distance to travel. They could spend it exploring and enjoying each other. And, if Labor Day loomed as a depressing dead end, she had to be optimistic. It might turn out to be no more than a temporary roadblock.

She dressed, pausing for a moment outside her door before turning toward the second story staircase. She found Jason in his room, still in bed, wearing nothing but his reading glasses. He was looking at a news magazine which he tossed aside when he noticed Rachel standing by the entryway.

"Thank you for the rose," she said.

"The truth is, I was thinking more about *my* comfort than *your* reputation when I left. From now on we sleep in the king-sized bed. But I didn't want you to feel abandoned. Come kiss me good morning."

Rachel sat down on the bed, bending down to give him a chaste peck on the lips. Jason yanked at her arm, catching her off-balance, and she wound up sprawled across his chest, half on top of him. The next moment she was flat on her back, pinned beneath Jason's body.

"You'll have to do better than that," he said.

"I'm a slow learner. Teach me."

He wasted no time with preliminary teasing. His tongue probed her mouth hungrily and she could feel the hardness of his body demanding that she yield. Rachel's own passion flared in response and she clasped her arms around his waist, trailing tickling fingers up and down his back, her intimate exploration exciting both of them.

Jason pulled his mouth away and raised himself up on one elbow to unbutton her blouse. "I thought you were demonstrating a good morning *kiss,*" Rachel teased.

"You've got the wrong noun," he growled back.

"I'd like to stay here all day." Jason stretched lazily, exuding an arrogant satisfaction which reminded Rachel of a Greek god, triumphant because the woman who had initially struggled against his embrace had ultimately surrendered with a moan of pleasure. Although Rachel certainly hadn't struggled she had most assuredly been pleased. Jason had been both tender and passionate, murmuring compliments to her beauty and sensuality that made her feel as irresistible as a Siren. He had made love to her not only with his body but with his mind.

She ran her hand up his arm and across his chest, enjoying the sense of ownership she felt. "You *do* have company," she reminded him.

"Correction. My *mother* has company. And not for long. I want to be alone with you, Rachel. I'm getting rid of them." He swung off the bed, looked in the direction of the bathroom and then grinned. "I was going to ask you to take a shower with me, but we'd probably never make it to breakfast. Wait for me?"

Rachel smilingly agreed, then dressed and straightened up the bedroom while Jason showered and shaved. Her reward for this piece of housework was a leisurely kiss. "Umm. That was nice," she said. "Next time you want to make love in the morning, shave first."

"Just like a woman. Take her to bed a few times and she figures she has the right to nag you." Rachel grabbed a pillow from the bed and raised it up to throw at him, but he was out the door before she released it. When she reached the top of the steps he was already halfway down; she heaved the pillow at his retreating back. Unfortunately, she miscalculated his speed, so that the pillow dropped ineffectually onto the second step just as he reached the bottom.

"I'll let you hit me with it if it'll make you feel better," he called up to her.

She sniffed that the whole argument was adolescent, retrieved the pillow and took it back to the bedroom. When she returned he was still waiting for her. "If you let me tear off your clothes again I'll shave first," he said, laughing.

Rachel smiled and continued down the steps, telling him she would think it over. They strolled into the dining room arm-in-arm. Paula Chapin, Lady Bennett and the Pollocks were seated at the table; Stephen, Paula remarked, was in the kitchen, cooking breakfast. Rachel was on her way inside when she caught Jason's drawled, "It's been a pleasure having all of you, but you're leaving this morning."

Lady Bennett cheerfully informed him that she was spending the rest of the week at the Foxworths and then returning to London. Rachel couldn't hear any more of the conversation; Stephen had clicked on the electric fan in the range hood to clear the room of the odor of frying bacon.

She watched him sprinkle cinnamon onto the French toast and then turn each piece. "Was Jason angry last night?" he asked.

"What do you think?"

"I couldn't tell. That's one of the reasons I want him in my play. He's a first-rate actor."

"You don't have to tell *me* that. Actually, it was just a game, but I never guessed, and I was so intent on not letting him intimidate me that he didn't realize I was scared out of my wits. But things got straightened out eventually."

"Which is why he's throwing us out," Stephen said. "I don't blame him, but do me a favor, Rachel. Work on him about the play."

She shook her head. She had more reason than anyone to want Jason in New York, but she wasn't about to become someone else's lobbyist. "You know I agree with you, Stephen, and Jason knows it, too. But I'm not going to pressure him. You've seen how he reacts. Anyway, it *is* his decision."

"I thought you'd say that," Stephen admitted. "But don't blame me for trying."

Rachel would have been surprised if he hadn't, given the insistence with which he had questioned her the night before, and told him so. Then she dispatched him into the dining room with a platter of French toast and bacon. As she finished cooking a second batch of each, the previously low-key conversation from next door erupted into angry shouting which was audible even above the whir of the electric fan.

"But you never stopped to think about that, did you?" The sarcastic question came from Stephen Chapin. "Are you going to stay up here and throw it all away? You used to take risks, damn you! You really let that bitch get to you, didn't you?"

Rachel hurriedly transferred the food to a serving dish and carried it into the dining room. Jason, looking furious, was yelling back at Stephen, "Don't you ever get tired of telling me how to live? I don't need your damn advice."

"Yeah? Suppose you'd listened to me when I told you to stay away from her? Your bloody life would have turned out better!"

"Now boys," Lady Bennett clucked, "you're allowing a difference of . . ."

"*You* keep out of this!" Jason snapped. "You've caused enough trouble, dragging half the world up here on some blasted crusade that's none of your business in the first place."

Lady Bennett disregarded this tirade with her usual unflappability. "I brought you Rachel," she pointed out with a smile.

Jason glared at his mother, swept a contemptuous gaze at the others in the room and stalked away from the table. A few seconds later they heard the sound of the front door slamming shut.

"That's getting to be a habit with him," Stephen remarked.

His wife shot him a disapproving look. "One of these days, Stephen, you're going to learn some tact. You can only push people so far before they turn and fight back."

"Thanks for the advice, Paula, but I told him what he needs to hear. He loves performing. He's letting his hang-ups get in the way of something he wants to do."

Obviously, Rachel told herself, Friday night's argument had been played out all over again. Stephen Chapin had about as much common sense as an amoeba. "Don't you think he knows that?" she asked him. "He has reasons for how he feels. They aren't trivial ones. Why couldn't you have left him alone?"

"Since when did *you* become his protector? Since you started sharing his bed?"

In twenty-eight years no one had attacked Rachel with such deliberate crudeness. If her first instinct was to bolt out of the room in embarrassment, her second was to dump the plate of French toast over his head. What restrained her was the knowledge that, to Stephen Chapin, she was the outsider here, a woman who barely knew Jason Wilder and thus had no right to comment on an argument between long-time friends.

"I happen to be in love with him, Stephen," she said. Her tone, though soft, left no doubt as to the intensity of her emotions. "That means I try to understand him. You're sitting there and telling yourself that what you've done is for Jason's own good, but I have to question that. If you cared about him you'd see that he can't handle the pressure right now. What concerns you is your play, not Jason's happiness."

Stephen stared at her in silent antagonism for several moments, then dropped his eyes to his plate, smiling slightly. "You happen to be very wrong, but you're also one hell of a lady." He glanced up at her. "If he lets you get away he's out of his mind. I'm sorry, Rachel. Can I clear the table in penance?"

"You can clean up the whole kitchen," she answered.

Paula Chapin burst out laughing. "That's the first time in four years that I can remember Stephen apologizing to anyone, Rachel," she said. "Last time, the man on the receiving end was a director and he was so stunned that he stood there with his mouth open." She looked at her husband. "If I were you, darling, I'd keep on her good side."

"I should have remembered the T.V. interviews before I opened my mouth," Stephen admitted. "I didn't have to understand Spanish to know you were formidable, Rachel." He got up to make more coffee, whistling to himself as he walked off to the kitchen.

They managed to finish their breakfast without further incident. Afterward, Rachel took pity on Stephen and helped him clean up. Now that both of them had cooled down they were able to talk about their argument. The conversation confirmed Rachel's earlier supposition as to Stephen's motive for his earlier comments to her.

As Jason's close friend for almost fourteen years

he felt he had the right—even the duty—to say things that other people shouldn't. Rachel's intervention had provoked him. "But Paula is right," he added. "Tact isn't my strong point. I get away with being abrasive because people who don't know me figure I'm a brilliant but eccentric playwright who has to be humored. And my friends are so used to it that they ignore it. To tell you the truth, I've seen Jason upset and I've seen him depressed, but I've never seen him so touchy."

"If the nerve is raw enough," Rachel answered, "most of us wince when it's jabbed at."

"Conflict about doing the play isn't the only thing that's bothering him." Stephen sprayed some liquid cleaner on the tile counter and wiped it away with a flourish. "Your work is in New York, Rachel. It's obvious that New Hampshire is too quiet for you. I pointed that out to Jason—one reason why he should do the play. He mumbled something about your giving up your business to write full time. So I asked him if he had talked it over with you. He dodged the question, just like I knew he would, and I lit into him. Obviously you heard that part of it. That's when all hell broke loose."

He took careful aim and shot the sponge into the sink. "I shouldn't have reminded him that I was right about Meredith, though. Even if it's true."

*That,* Rachel thought, was an understatement. "He told me you were there when he needed someone. How do you think it made him feel to have you pat yourself on the back for being such a smart guy?"

Stephen poured himself another cup of coffee and sat down on a kitchen stool. "You're thinking that I have about as much finesse as a truck, and you're dead right. I'm probably lucky nobody's shot me yet. But I meant what I told you, Rachel. You're a terrific lady. Jason needs someone like you, someone who can be an equal partner, to share his life and support him. Anyone as close to his emotions as Jason is bleeds too easily. If you define strength as the ability to distance yourself from strong feelings and get on with living, Jason isn't strong—not like you are."

He set his cup on the counter. Rachel, who had been standing in the middle of the kitchen, pulled over a stool and sat down next to him. "Let me tell you about Meredith Lloyd, Rachel," Stephen continued. "She manipulated other people by being helpless. Jason got sucked into feeling responsible for her and it damn near destroyed him. He's been retreating from life ever since, pouring his emotions into his books instead of into people. That may be good for his readers, but it's lousy for him. Then he met you and he was smart enough to see that you're right for him. I want him to be happy, Rachel. He's my friend and, regardless of what you think, my motives weren't only self-serving."

"I know that. If I hadn't been angry I wouldn't have said what I did." Talking as much to herself as to Stephen, Rachel went on, "But what you said about me—that I was strong—I've never seen myself that way."

Until listening to Stephen Rachel hadn't realized just how deeply Jason's first marriage had scarred him. Now she understood that he hadn't fallen in love with her because of the book he had written. On the contrary, the last thing he wanted was to become involved with another Meredith—or Maria. What he saw as Rachel's strength and independence was precisely what had attracted him.

"It's not easy to turn your life around the way you've done," Stephen answered. "People spend years in therapy with only the barest change in their behavior to show for it. You condemn yourself because it was difficult and because there were setbacks. But put almost anyone under enough stress and he'll crack. That's not weakness, Rachel. That's being human."

Rachel leaned over and kissed him on the cheek. "Thank you, Stephen. You've helped me see things I couldn't," she said.

Her expression of gratitude appeared to embarrass Stephen, who changed the subject by asking when she would be returning to New York. They wound up exchanging phone numbers and addresses before he went upstairs to help Paula pack.

Thinking about Jason, Rachel realized that she had sensed his vulnerability many times. But having grown up with the notion that men reined in whatever emotions they felt and dominated their women in return for offering protection she had automatically tried to fit Jason into the same mold. She had attributed any aberrant behavior to the fact that he loved her, not to a difference in his essential nature.

That, of course, was nonsense. Like most people, Jason wanted his own way, but his ability to see all points of view repeatedly pulled him in the direction of accomodation. When he appeared to be detached it was invariably an act. He was actually very emotional. She finally acknowledged that she had fallen in love with him for precisely these reasons. It wasn't enough that he understand her. She had needed a man who didn't seek to dominate her. She had needed someone whose openness and easy expression of emotion would gain her trust. And besides, Rachel thought with a smile, it hadn't hurt that he was the sexiest man on the entire North American continent.

When Jason returned to the house everyone was sitting in the living room, waiting to say good-bye to him. Jackie Pollock had decided to visit the Foxworths with Lady Bennett; the two women would then drive to New York together in the rented car. Lady Bennett, convinced that she had achieved the beginning of Jason's redemption, planned to fly back to London over the weekend, pick up her daughter, and then continue on to the south of France for the rest of the summer.

As they were loading the luggage into the cars Stephen Chapin drawled at Jason, "See you in December when we start rehearsals."

Jason's reaction was to grin at Stephen and call him a rude name, then embrace him. "Put in a few nude scenes and half a dozen aliens and maybe I'll change my mind," he laughed.

He enfolded his mother in a hug, then wished everyone else a safe trip. As the cars disappeared down the driveway he took Rachel's hand and led her back to the house.

"I've been doing some thinking," he told her. "I want you to know that I'm aware of the impasse we seem to have reached. You need people and activity around you. Give me a week in New York with your kind of stimulation and all I can think about is going home, away from the noise and the dirt and the crowds and the people who stop me for autographs. What I *don't* know is what we do about it."

"We have three weeks together," Rachel answered. "Can we forget about the future, just for three weeks?" She slid her arms around his neck. "Let's just love each other, Jason."

He bent his head to kiss her lightly on the mouth. "Are you telling me you don't have any more doubts about how you feel?"

She nodded. "Not after talking to Stephen. He may be a pain in the neck at times, but he helped me understand our relationship. You can make fun of me, but I feel as though we're good for each other."

"You don't *feel* it. You've decided to *think* it. But I'm not going to complain, except about owing Chapin even more than I used to."

"He's your friend. He cares about you."

"I know that. And maybe he's right. Maybe all of you are right. But I can't face the three ring circus, Rachel. The mobs of people and the media hype and the lack of privacy—I can't deal with it."

"I understand," Rachel answered. And she did, having lived through several weeks of it herself. She didn't want to think about the future, just savor the sweetness of the present.

The next week was like a honeymoon. Jason put aside his book to take Rachel on a series of short trips throughout the surrounding area. On Monday they drove up through the White Mountains to Franconia Notch and then Mt. Washington, the highest point in the east. The next day they traveled over to the coast to Portsmouth to tour the historic homes there and then stayed at Hampton Beach till

Thursday. They visited Hanover and Dartmouth College, where several friends of Jason's were professors, and enjoyed the Marlboro Music Festival in southern Vermont over the weekend. They talked and laughed, ate more than they should have and made love whenever the mood hit them, which was often.

Rachel had received several more letters from Susan, but couldn't figure out just what sort of relationship existed between her sister and Kenny Brownlow, the California college teacher she had met. Susan's letters were full of the man, but there was no indication that they were actually lovers.

Since Susan was due back to New York on Thursday, Rachel called that evening to find out if she could spend the following week in New Hampshire. Rachel was very open about her relationship with Jason, but Susan said little either about Kenny or the trip. She sounded tired, which might have accounted for her unusual reticence.

"It was hectic," she said. "I could use a rest, but I wouldn't want to intrude . . ."

Rachel started to laugh. "Jason's beginning to talk about his book again. I can see he's itching to get back to work, but he promised me he would take a week off and he's being very good about it. I'll be glad to have some company next week."

In fact, Jason bounded out of bed at seven o'clock Monday morning and, when Rachel sleepily followed half an hour later, she found him sitting at his typewriter, rereading the most recently written pages of manuscript. "This needs work," he muttered. "Make me breakfast, Rachel?"

"Together only a week and already you're treating me like the cook again," she pouted.

193

He looked up at her, his expression distracted. "You know I'm crazy about you. But it's a matter of specialization. You cook better than I do."

Rachel retorted that she would be delighted to give him lessons, whereupon he offered to cook dinner, knowing full well that Rachel would never subject Susan to one of his experiments. Defeated, but not minding it, she went downstairs to the kitchen.

After a week of continual activity the day passed far too slowly. Rachel tried to resume her original schedule of riding, shopping, sunbathing and reading, but was so restless that she drove to Lebanon early in the afternoon and prowled around the town until it was time to meet Susan's plane. By the time she spotted her sister she was wondering whether she could have survived for another two weeks without some company.

They hugged, then inspected each other. Each thought that the other looked marvelous. On the way home Susan started talking about her trip to France, broadcasting a self-confidence which had been absent when she left. Having lived in Paris for a year Susan spoke passable French, and knew the surrounding countryside much better than any of the others had. She was the one who had planned both where they went and what they saw and had also taken the lead in dealing with obstreperous innkeepers and rude waiters.

Her relationship with Kenny Brownlow had stopped short of an affair, and yet enough had happened between them so that Susan thought of it as a romance. Rachel could see that another man's interest had done her sister a lot of good. She had realized, she told Rachel, that she wanted to attempt a reconciliation with Philip. If his attitude hadn't changed in the last eighteen months, however, she was prepared to file for divorce. She would no longer live her life in limbo.

When Susan first met Jason her attitude was one of wariness bordering on hostility. Although she accepted the fact that Rachel loved him she still thought of him as the man whose book had caused her sister months of anguish and depression. Understanding her distrust, Jason took the time to talk about his feelings, his sincerity and emotion so palpable that Susan ended up apologizing for misjudging him.

Now that Susan was keeping her company much of Rachel's restlessness had vanished. When they weren't horseback riding or sightseeing they were cooking. A busy schedule in New York had left no time for testing unusual recipes that no one would ever request, but up here in New Hampshire they were able to indulge their passion for experimentation. Sometimes the results were noble failures, but no one went hungry.

Susan's relationship with Jason deepened as the days passed, a development which pleased Rachel very much. Susan was frank in talking about Philip and her marriage, but then, Jason had a talent for drawing people out. The first night of Susan's visit he had explained that he knew her husband and given Susan his impressions. Toward the end of the week he suggested to her that Philip might spend a few days in New Hampshire, talking to her about their marriage away from the pressures of their dual careers.

"That's three against one," Susan said. "He won't like the odds."

"Never mind what Philip wants. What do *you* want?" Jason asked.

"Philip is very good at convincing people that his point of view is the only one that makes sense. I've gained a lot of confidence since we separated, but I'm not ready to take him on alone." Susan looked over at Rachel, her eyes defensive. "I know I should be able to face him myself, Rachel, but I . . ."

"*I* never said so. Don't be such a martyr, Suzy. There's nothing wrong with needing some help."

There was a telephone sitting on the end table next to the couch and Rachel picked up the receiver, wiggling it in the air. "Who's going to make the call?"

Jason was soon selected, the rationale being that, as host of this would-be reunion, he should issue the invitation. In fact, all of them knew he would do the best job of handling Philip Lenglen.

Susan told him Philip's phone number, adding that if he wasn't at home the call would automatically be switched to his answering service. She was pleating the bottom of her tee shirt as Jason punched the buttons.

He listened a moment, then placed a hand over the receiver. "It's the service," he said. "I'd like to leave a message for Dr. Lenglen," he continued into the phone. "Please have him call Jason Wilder immediately. I'm at home in New Hampshire, and the number is (603) 555–0538." There was a brief pause. "No, it isn't a joke." A second pause, accompanied by an exasperated frown. "You could try listening to my voice. Do you want me to recite my opening lines from *Parallel Universe* for you?"

Rachel couldn't help smiling and was punished for this offense by a moody stare from Jason. "Right," he said. "Yeah, it's okay. Forget it. Just tell Dr. Lenglen that I'll be in all night." He hung up the telephone.

"Does that happen often?" Susan asked, sounding awe-struck.

"Often enough when I'm calling someone I don't know. I've even had people hang up on me." He slumped back against the cushions of the couch, groaning. "Ten to one I read in the papers that Jason Wilder is thinking about a face lift. Why couldn't you have married an allergist, Suzy?"

When the phone rang some fifteen minutes later Jason picked it up, crisply informing Philip that Rachel and Susan were in New Hampshire and that his wife wanted him to come up for the weekend. The invitation was apparently followed by several questions from Philip, because Jason kept putting him off. Finally he said firmly, "It's a complicated situation, Philip. I'll be glad to talk to you about it if you want to come up here. Like I told you, Susan would like to see you, but she doesn't want to see you alone." He paused, then held out the phone to Susan. "He wants to speak to you."

Susan's hand was trembling as she accepted the receiver. She listened for a few moments, then replied, "If that's what I wanted I would have gone to see a lawyer, Philip. I want to work things out, but there have to be some changes." Rachel watched her sister's face redden with embarrassment. "I don't know. We'll talk about it when you get here."

She handed the phone back to Jason, who started to give Philip directions to Linwood. "What did he say?" Rachel hissed.

"He wanted to know if we were going to share a bedroom. He said he didn't think he could stand to spend the weekend here if I wasn't going to let him touch me."

"And?"

"You know I love him. It's been eighteen months, Rachel."

"You don't have to justify it to *me,*" Rachel smiled. "I know you and Philip had problems, but that wasn't one of them."

"No," Susan said, looking worried. "It wasn't, was it?"

# Chapter Ten

$\mathcal{P}$hilip arrived several hours ahead of schedule on Friday. Rachel and Susan had gone riding and were walking back from the stables when his yellow Porsche pulled up to the front walk. His eagerness, Rachel decided, was a good sign.

The first thing she noticed when Philip got out of the car was the contrast between his appearance and her sister's. Susan was tanned and healthy-looking. After several days of rest in New Hampshire the fatigue from her hectic two and a half weeks in France was gone. She had let her hair grow out several inches since separating from Philip and the disarrayed blond curls were streaked from exposure to the summer sunshine. As for Susan's enviable curves, the halter top and jeans she wore did nothing to conceal them.

Philip, on the other hand, looked tense and tired.

He had always been a handsome man, about six feet tall with a lithe and rangy build, dark brown hair, blue eyes and a smile that radiated sympathy and confidence. Now, however, his expression was defensive and unsmiling. The tan suit he wore, though beautifully tailored, hung a little too loosely on his body. Obviously the last eighteen months had been as difficult for him as they had been for Susan.

Susan carried off the unavoidably awkward greeting with far more aplomb than did Philip. She managed a smile and told him, "You've lost weight in eighteen months. I can see you've missed my cooking."

"I've missed *you*," he answered. Although he avoided Susan's eyes he couldn't seem to tear his gaze away from her body.

Rachel, whose relationship with her brother-in-law had always been up front, said bluntly, "You're looking at her like you want to carry her up to the bedroom and devour her. Weren't there any women in Boston, Philip?"

He frowned. Rachel, rather relieved, saw some of the arrogance she had come to expect from him in that disapproving look of his. "That's none of your damn business," he snapped.

Suitably assured that Dr. Philip Lenglen was far from a beaten man, Rachel couldn't help but be amused by his behavior. He might be nervous about the prospect of spending a weekend with three people whom he perceived as critics, if not precisely enemies, but that didn't mean he planned to retreat behind a series of mea culpas. He pulled his suitcase out of the back seat of the Porsche, saying to Susan, "This is the weirdest situation I've ever found myself in. I don't like walking into something that feels like a court martial. And, for your sister's information, there were plenty of women in Boston, but not for the last six months." He glared at Rachel, who smiled back. "Satisfied?"

"Obviously *you're* not." She giggled.

For a moment he seemed ready to throw the suitcase back into the car and drive straight home to Boston, but the mood passed almost immediately. He started to laugh, shaking his head. "You know, it's good to see you looking so good, Rachel," he said. He dropped the suitcase and gave her a hug. "What are you doing with Jason Wilder? I thought you hated the guy."

"We'll tell you about it after you get settled." Rachel cocked her head toward Susan. "Aren't you going to kiss your wife hello?"

Philip looked uncertainly at Susan, who held out her arms. Rachel walked away, saying she would see them later. When she glanced back from the doorway of the house they were tangled in a passionate embrace.

She went upstairs to tell Jason that Philip had arrived only to find him watching the ongoing reunion from one of the dormer windows. Philip was still holding Susan in his arms, but her hands were resting against his chest, as if to prevent closer contact. Whatever he was saying met with her disapproval, because she kept shaking her head. Finally he nodded and dropped his arms to his sides. Susan started into the house and Philip followed, looking less than happy.

"We see before us a rejected man," Jason said with a grin.

"You can't expect my sister to hop into bed with him after eighteen months—not after everything that's happened," Rachel answered.

"Regardless of her reasons, it's sensible strategy." Jason took Rachel's hand and led her toward the steps. "It's time for me to play the gracious host, Rachel."

They intercepted Susan and Philip in the second story hall. Jason shook hands with the latter, making easy conversation about Paul Rideau's progress. Philip, the neutral topic relaxing him, remarked, "I should stop by to see him while I'm up here. It'll save him a trip to New York."

None of them missed the fact that he had said "New York" rather than "Boston," indicating that he had already decided where he would open a practice. But no one followed up on the comment. By mutual, if unspoken, agreement they left talk of the future for later.

"How about now?" Jason asked Philip. "Give him a call to make sure he's home, then I'll drive over with you. You can use the phone in the master bedroom." Without waiting for an answer he picked up Philip's suitcase and carried it toward the bedroom. Susan, who was sleeping in Rachel's former room, took her sister's arm to prevent her from following the two men.

"I want to get something to drink," she said. "Come down to the kitchen with me."

Downstairs, Susan took a pitcher of iced tea out of the refrigerator while Rachel filled two glasses with crushed ice. When they were seated at the counter with their drinks Susan told her in a disbelieving tone, "He really expected to come up here and drag me off to bed and then live happily ever after. He

202

used to do that when we'd have a fight. He'd make love to me and it would be so terrific that I wouldn't want to argue anymore. But I'm not going to let him get away with that kind of sexual blackmail now and I told him so. You know Philip—the best defense is a good offense. He had the nerve to accuse me of being a tease."

"So what did you say? Did you tell him he was full of baloney?"

Susan nodded her head vigorously. "You'd better believe it! I'm not letting him make love to me unless I think we have a chance of working things out. I don't need that kind of temptation."

Rachel agreed with Susan's stance in the matter and told her so. She also mentioned Jason's comment that saying "No" was sensible strategy. "I suppose he meant that Philip will never think about changing until he's convinced that it's the only way to get what he wants. But you know something, Suzy? Even if he finally figures out that he'd be happier if he were more open and makes some real progress at it, he'll still want to be the boss."

"He's going to find that it won't be so easy now," Susan answered. "I realize that I have to stand up to him."

It was exactly what Rachel had hoped Susan would say. In spite of the fact that Philip had unconsciously pushed her into it he had been shocked when Susan walked out and refused to return. He had to understand that just because she was the one who had initiated this attempted reconciliation it didn't mean that she was crawling back to him.

Shortly thereafter Philip and Jason stopped into the kitchen to say they were leaving. Rachel, thinking that a gentle atmosphere might be a good idea on the first night of Philip's visit, suggested a gourmet dinner complete with music and candlelight.

"He'll accuse me of teasing him again," Susan pointed out, more than a little amused.

"Good!" Rachel retorted. "Let him suffer a little. He'll survive it."

The two men returned several hours later and walked straight into the kitchen, following their noses with as much acumen as Synge followed his. Jason proceeded to lift a pair of saucepan covers. "Chinese?" he asked.

"Eight courses worth," Susan answered, "and some of it is hot enough to melt your tastebuds."

"I knew there was *another* reason I came up here," Philip said with a smile.

The tension which had been so obvious only a few hours ago now seemed to have vanished. Rachel wondered what Philip and Jason had talked about during their drive to Lebanon and back. They seemed on the friendliest of terms.

Her question was answered almost as soon as they sat down to dinner. "You've been listening to me drone on about my cases for the last couple of hours," Philip remarked to Jason. "But what I really want to know is, how did you and Rachel meet up with each other?"

The brief outline initially offered by Rachel gradually grew into a complex discussion of feelings and motivations. Philip's fascination was as unexpected as it was intense. The man Rachel had known two years ago had been scientific and analytical. He had refused to listen to Susan's talk of emotions and needs, putting all areas of disagreement into a logical framework that he alone had permission to define or modify. His brilliance as a debater had invariably won every argument, but, in the end, his rational approach had been an empty exercise. Susan had listened to her instincts instead of his logic.

During the eighteen months of their separation he had apparently discovered that people sometimes acted in ways that he considered irrational and, indeed, that a course of action which he perceived as sensible might even be a mistake for the person involved. He had even figured out that apparent and actual motivations could differ radically.

The conversation lasted until long past midnight because time and again Philip prolonged it. Two subjects intrigued him in particular. First, he wanted to hear about Rachel's sessions with Dr. Quinby and to understand the process whereby she had so radically changed her lifestyle and then gradually put her past behind her. Her inability to define precise milestones frustrated him and he constantly probed at her emotions, thereby frustrating *her*.

"What do you mean, you don't know how you felt?" he asked at one point. "How can you not know?"

"I just don't, that's all!" Rachel snapped back. "It's easy enough to define your feelings if you don't *have* any. You just take a logical look at what a so-called normal person in your situation should feel and tell yourself that that's what *you* feel, too. But *real* feelings tend to be more complex than that. Even though I spent a lot of time *trying* to figure things out I was too confused to really understand *what* was going on in my head."

Philip ignored her outburst and continued with his questions, in due course arriving at the second subject of fascination: the evolving relationship between Rachel and Jason. "So you don't think of her as 'Maria' anymore?" he asked toward the end of the evening.

"I can't separate the two," Jason answered. "If I were a scientist, like you are, Philip, I would come up with something like, 'The potential that attracted me to Rachel four years ago has now realized itself in a completely positive way,' but frankly, I don't give a damn about that. What's important to me is how I feel and I don't need to analyze it down to the last molecule to know that I love her."

"Atom," Philip said with a grin. "Neutrino. Quark."

"You should get together with your sister-in-law," Jason drawled. "The two of you would spend so much time picking apart motivations that you'd forget people are supposed to enjoy each other."

He rose, stretched and reached out a hand to Rachel, pulling her up from the couch. "We'll see you two in the morning," he said, slipping an arm around her waist.

As they were walking toward the door they heard Philip ask Susan in a husky tone of voice, "Come to bed, Suzy?"

Her answer was loud enough to reach them in the hallway. "First we lay out the ground rules, Philip. Ask me again tomorrow."

Rachel and Jason exchanged a smile that grew into outright laughter by the time they reached the bedroom. "Philip gave a good performance tonight, but he looked at your sister every time he thought no one would notice. The poor guy is in agony," Jason said. "Or at least, he's as much in agony as someone that closed off from his emotions can possibly be.

But he knows he's got a problem, which is more than he knew a few years ago. We talked about some of his cases this afternoon. He told me he'd had an affair with one of his colleagues, a woman about ten years older than he is. She accused him of all the same things that you and your sister did and it got through to that analytical mind of his that maybe all of you had a point. That was six months ago. He hasn't gone out since then, maybe to punish himself for the affair, or maybe just to prove to himself that he wants Susan and no one else. I think his celibacy just caught up with him."

"Don't be such a cynic," Rachel said, starting to undress. "I think he's made some real progress. I'm surprised he was open enough to tell you as much as he did, though." She paused thoughtfully, then added, "Not that I should be. I used to wonder how you had gotten people in Santandia to talk to you. But I've seen you in action with Susan and Philip and even me, and you have the most incredible ability to make people trust you. It even comes across on a movie screen."

"Wait until tomorrow night before you credit me with superhuman powers," Jason answered. "Philip was comfortable tonight because I promised him we'd stay away from the subject of him and Susan. Put him in the hot seat and he'll either clam up or counterattack."

He snatched away the nightgown that Rachel was about to pull over her head and dropped it to the floor, then picked her up and tossed her onto the bed. "About my ability to inspire trust," he murmured, sitting down next to her. He bent his head to tease a nipple with his mouth, biting it gently. "You never tell me what you like in bed."

A low ache permeated Rachel's body and she ran her hands over the muscles in Jason's back, massaging them possessively. "I like whatever you do," she said.

Jason lay down beside her and nuzzled his way up her neck, stopping after a few maddening passes at her mouth. "Cop-out," he whispered.

"I like to be surprised."

He shook his head. "Not good enough."

Rachel felt her face reddening. "Jason, please . . ."

"Do you like this?" His hand feathered down her side to her inner thigh, the half-tickle, half-caress arousing her wildly. "Or this?" His hand became more intimate, touching her lightly, teasingly, causing her to arch her body in frustration.

"Yes." The admission was a breathless one. Rachel sought his mouth, only to be punished with several more butterfly-light kisses.

"Stop that," she moaned.

"How do you want me to kiss you?"

"Not like that."

"How then?"

"You know how."

He rolled away from her, sprawling onto his back, and then stared at the ceiling as if he had committed some unforgivable offense. Rachel was puzzled by his moodiness. Surely her responses told him what pleased her most even if her words didn't.

She snuggled up against his side and nuzzled his neck with her lips. "It just embarrasses me to put it into words, Jason. That doesn't mean I don't trust you."

He looked more troubled than angry after this admission. Rachel knew that something was bothering him, but when she asked him what it was he simply shook his head. She started to move away, thinking he wanted to be alone, but his arm immediately snaked itself around her body, keeping her close beside him.

She wasn't capable of reeling off her preferences like some talking sexual handbook, but her intuition denied that that could be the real issue here. Since Jason already knew what excited her it had to be her failure to convey her feelings that disturbed him. He was always telling her he loved her and whispering compliments to her sensuality, but she never returned the favor.

Smiling to herself, she ran teasing fingers across his stomach and brushed her lips against his mouth. "You have the sexiest skin," she murmured. "Smooth, hard"—her tongue tasted the area just below his ear—"and salty. I have dangerously possessive feelings about you. If you were ever unfaithful to me I'd want to strangle both of you."

She looked into Jason's eyes, seeing both amusement and pleasure there. Thus encouraged, she continued with several more compliments, each more intimate than the last, and was rewarded by the slowly growing smile which eventually took over his face. After one outrageously flamboyant phrase —something about an intrepid explorer in the Amazon jungle—both of them burst out laughing.

"That *is* what you wanted, then?" Rachel asked. "To hear me *say* how I feel instead of having to figure it out from my actions?"

"Is that so surprising? I make my living with words. Until just now I didn't realize how important it is to . . ."

"How utterly pompous," Rachel interrupted with

another giggle. "It's just that your enormous male ego needs stroking, not that you're a writer."

"My 'enormous male ego,' huh?" Jason started to kiss her, obviously intending to torment her as revenge for her mockery, but quickly surrendered to more urgent needs. As always, the contained explosiveness of his lovemaking overwhelmed Rachel and forced her into a hungry kind of submissiveness. Feeling her excitement, Jason broke the kiss to whisper against her lips, "If you're looking for something to stroke I can think of better things than my ego."

As aroused as Rachel was nothing could have induced her to pass up such an obvious opportunity to tease him. She trailed light kisses to his ear, nibbled at the lobe and then murmured seductively, "You have the most exciting ego of any man I've ever met, Jason. Firm, hard, and dangerous. The minute I met you, I knew . . ."

"Oh, be quiet." He laughed, silencing her with a hard kiss. He pulled her close against his side, alternately arousing and demanding, making love to her with a smoldering passion that obviated the need for words.

After breakfast on Saturday Jason suggested that they spend the day in the resort area of Lake Winnipesaukee in the eastern part of New Hampshire. He avoided the highway in favor of a back route through White Mountain forests and alongside charging, rock-littered streams. Most of the afternoon was taken up with a cruise on an excursion steamer which circled the lake, one of the largest bodies of water in New England.

During their previous sightseeing Rachel had either been alone with Jason in his car, walking along at a pace that discouraged familiarity, listening to a concert or watching a film. People would come up to Jason, ask for an autograph and then go about their business.

Now, however, they were in the company of a large, contained group of people who had nothing to do with themselves but eat, talk and watch the scenery go by. Given three hours on a boat with Jason Wilder, it was astonishing how many of them came up to shake his hand, ask for autographs or merely gawk, then stayed either to question him or for some impenetrable purpose of their own.

The situation made Jason uncomfortable. His sense of responsibility was at war with his sense of privacy. Anyone else would have either ignored the worst of the fans or told them exactly where to go, but Jason seemed unable to manage either course of action. Several times he dodged appallingly personal questions with flip answers or witty combacks, looking almost guilty for not telling these strangers the story of his life. Even the majority of the fans, who were polite, complimentary and brief, seemed to make him uneasy. He reminded Rachel of a cornered animal.

He only enjoyed himself with the children. They were only too quick to tell him that he was older, shorter and less tough-looking than on the screen. Their innocent complaints genuinely delighted him and he would kneel down to their level and spin stories from his work on the *Parallel Universe* trilogy that sent them skipping away either awed or giggling.

At first Rachel felt that Jason had to be left alone to handle his fans as best he could. But when a disagreeable woman charged up to him and demanded to know why his wife had killed herself Rachel couldn't hold her tongue. With a voice as chilly as Mt. Washington and eyes that caused the woman to back up a few steps she said, "It was an accident. She was a very disturbed woman."

She took Jason's arm and turned him toward the shoreline, ostensibly to point out a church they were passing. She wondered if he would upbraid her for interfering, but instead he gave her a pained smile and murmured, "I love you, tigress."

Rachel used her icy style of protectiveness three more times that afternoon, probably making an equal number of enemies. She didn't care at all. Her reward was that Jason's discomfort eased just a little.

The same scenario was repeated that afternoon and evening when they stopped into an agricultural fair in nearby Laconia. Now that Jason could keep moving he was more patient and comfortable. Nonetheless, when they were attacked on the way to the car by yet another gaggle of giggling teenaged girls it was all he could do to sign their pieces of paper and come up with some patter worthy of Hamlin Stone. Several weeks ago, Rachel recalled, she had thought to herself that Jason Wilder would never be uneasy or out of place no matter what the situation. She had been wrong.

"If I weren't making so much money from owning a percentage of those damn movies," he said as they got into the car, "I might even wish they would stop re-releasing them every year. People never forget— and they won't let me forget, either."

His comment was an allusion to his refusal to accept the lead in Stephen Chapin's play. Since

Rachel doubted that he actually wanted to discuss that she limited her reply to a teasing comment that he was hardly so big a star that he would be mobbed on the streets of New York.

"You're wrong," Philip stated with his usual assertiveness. "You should have seen the nurses in the hospital when he'd come to visit Paul. It isn't just the movies, or even that his books have been both best sellers and controversial. It's that he's refused to grant interviews and chosen to live in a relatively inaccessible place. A whole mystique has developed around him. Suzy told me about the play this morning, Jason. If you decide to do it you have to be ready for a three-ring circus."

"*I* know that, even if Stephen doesn't," Jason answered. "Let's talk about something else, like you and Susan."

Susan was sitting next to Rachel in the back seat, with Philip next to Jason, who was driving. Rachel could sense her sister's tension even before seeing it in her face.

Philip lit a cigarette and took a long drag. "All right. I suppose that's why I'm up here. Suzy? Are you going to list all my faults, besides the obvious ones? It was stupid to have an affair, I admit that. I hurt you and I'm sorry. But I've gotten it out of my system now. It's been months since I've touched another woman because I knew I was coming back to New York and I wanted to be with you."

"Your definition of 'being together' and my definition of it have never been the same." Susan's voice, at first low and tentative, gradually picked up strength. "I *do* love you, Philip. And I think I'm capable of putting the past behind me. I know you have the capacity to care about people because I've seen it with your patients and even with Rachel, when you got her to make the appointment with Dr. Quinby. But when someone gets too close to you it seems to threaten you. I was never sure how much you really loved me."

"Couldn't you tell how I felt by the way I made love to you? Why won't you let me show you?"

Susan looked at Rachel, exasperated. "It isn't enough, Philip. You use sex as a pacifier. That part of our marriage was always fine, but you never *talked* to me."

"I told you about my cases."

"But not how you felt about them. It was all technical, like you were giving me a lecture."

"What really bugs you is the business about your job," Philip said. "I was wrong about that; I admit it. My mother always worked and I wanted you home, that's all. I didn't take your training and your needs into account, but now I will."

Rachel listened with increasing despair as the conversation continued. Susan continually raised the issue of Philip's emotional distance, coming at the subject from half a dozen different angles. Philip would pin her down to a specific complaint, then either promise to remedy it, deny that there was a problem or subtly change the subject. Susan was perceptive enough to see the pattern and eventually started to repeat herself in an attempt to make him confront the subject. He countered by pretending that he really didn't understand her feelings, drawing her out until they were talking about her instead of him. Rachel was sure that his "interest" was just another avoidance technique.

An hour and a half later they walked into the house. Everyone knew exactly how Susan felt, but

Philip's feelings were as much of a mystery as ever. Jason led them into the living room, went into the library to fetch a bottle of brandy and then held it up. Philip nodded; Rachel and Susan shook their heads.

Susan and Rachel sat down together on the couch; the men took the armchairs to their left. "Look," Jason said to Philip, "you're a smart guy. You've got to be aware of what you're doing. When we talked yesterday afternoon you told me you understood you had a problem letting yourself get close to people. So why have you been stonewalling Susan for the last two hours?"

Philip's response was a twenty-five minute discourse about his childhood that would have melted an iceberg. His parents were distant, he said. They used love to manipulate him, rewarding him with approval when he pleased them and punishing him with coldness when he didn't. But they were also inconsistent in their actions, so that he never knew quite what to expect from them. He had learned not to trust people and was afraid to give anyone else the kind of power his parents had once held over him. He felt comfortable only when he was in control of situations, as he was when dealing with his patients.

"I can become involved with them and still feel safe," he explained. Rachel, listening to Philip's tone, studying his face, picked up a definite change in manner as he murmured the last sentence, then paused. Her brother-in-law invariably exercised such careful control over his feelings and conversation that one often had the sense that he was talking and observing himself at the same time.

Now Rachel probed Philip's features for some sign of that customary wariness and failed to discover it.

Either he was now able to rival Jason Wilder's acting ability or he had dropped the façade and was speaking from the heart.

"I operated on a teenaged girl earlier this summer," he continued, looking at Susan as he spoke. "Her case was the worst I've ever come across. No one wanted to touch it. It was as though the bones under her face couldn't agree on how fast to grow and had chosen different rates—her features were horribly twisted out of shape. When you look like that people either stare at you or turn away, appalled. They tend to assume that there's something wrong with your mind as well as your looks. Correcting it was going to involve breaking the underlying bones and resetting them, cutting away excess bone in some places and inserting a new artificial bone mixture we've been experimenting with in others—basically sculpting her whole facial structure. It took a lot of preparation before we were ready to go ahead and I got to know Chris and her parents very well."

He shook his head, as though lacking words with which to describe the family. "I've never met people like those parents, especially the mother. Their daughter looked freakish, but they had given her so much love . . . so much faith . . . Chris should have had ten dozen emotional problems, but she didn't. She had friends; she went to a regular school; she took part in school activities. People had obviously learned to regard her as almost normal. The parents accomplished that . . . combined with her own internal strength, of course. Some of my colleagues like to say that love is the most potent healing force on earth. Maybe they have a point."

"Was the surgery successful?" Susan asked.

From the way Philip smiled Rachel knew the case had touched him deeply. "She showed me a picture from a teen magazine the night before the operation —some sixteen-year-old T.V. star—and asked if I could make her look like that. I said I couldn't—the other girl's face was perfect—but that she would be . . . attractive. And she is. It was enormously satisfying to help someone as beautiful as Chris has always been, inside. She was in for a check-up last week and I hated the thought that I wouldn't see her again. It scared me to feel that way. It's never happened before. Usually I'm relieved when a case is finished."

"Are you trying to tell me? . . ." Susan checked herself, saying instead, "What are you trying to say?"

"That I'd feel safer picking up where we left off. It's what I would have done if you'd been willing. But being without you, and knowing Chris and her parents and other people like them, has taught me something about love, sharing, support, whatever you call it. After thirty-three years I understand that I've been missing something, but Suzy, I resent it. I was getting along fine. It was comfortable the old way. I don't want to need you or anyone else."

Jason got to his feet, walked over to Rachel and held out his hand to pull her up. Then, standing arm in arm with her, he said to Philip and Susan, "I think that the two of you finally have something to discuss. Suzy?"

"Yes. Good-night." Susan looked almost dejected as she murmured her reply. But as Rachel and Jason started out of the room, she added more cheerfully, "Rome wasn't built in a day, was it?"

Upstairs, lying in bed, Rachel snuggled into the

crook of Jason's arm and admitted that she had found the evening an exhausting one.

"It could have been a lot worse," he answered. "Philip understands the conflict he's feeling and he understands where it comes from. A part of him wants the love he's so afraid of. What happens now is up to him—and your sister."

"I think Suzy knows that. Fortunately, she wouldn't want Philip to turn into a seething bundle of emotions. That type of man doesn't attract her."

"And you?" Jason growled. "What attracts you?"

Rachel chose to answer with actions rather than words.

# Chapter Eleven

$W$hen Rachel and Jason passed by Susan's bedroom early the next morning they noticed that the bed inside showed no sign of use. Smiling at each other, they continued down to the kitchen, only to find Susan sitting at the counter, dressed in jeans and a turtleneck, drinking coffee. Rachel began to think that her sister had simply stayed up all night, but soon realized she was wrong. Susan blushed like a teenager the moment Jason shot her his best lecherous look, complete with slyly cocked eyebrow.

"Tough night, huh, Suzy?" he teased.

"We talked for three hours. And that was the *easy* part."

Rachel immediately suggested that she and Susan ride into town for the Sunday paper. "I'll go throw on some clothes." She grinned at Jason. "*You* can cook breakfast for a change."

Although Jason returned a comment to the effect

that the Grant sisters' assertiveness threatened to unman the world's entire male population, his simultaneous wink conveyed his sensitivity to Susan and Rachel's desire to spend some time alone, talking.

As the two women drove into Linwood Susan admitted to Rachel that her conversation with Philip hadn't been easy at all. "It's not very pleasant to sit there and hear about the competition, even though I tell myself that none of them meant anything to him and that he probably even learned something during our separation. At least he was jealous of Kenny, though. He was shocked to find out that I'd let any other man lay a hand on me."

"Fine. It's about time he realized it," Rachel replied. "But really, Suzy, I think that other women are the least of your troubles. Maybe Philip was trying to convince himself that someone else would do just as well as you, but it's obvious that he realizes now that that isn't true. You're the one he wants to be with."

"That's what I tell myself. He didn't sound as though he'd been happy during the last eighteen months. Mostly we talked about what we'd both done, how we thought we'd changed." Susan went on to repeat much of the conversation to Rachel, filling her in on the specifics of Philip's life: his professional and personal relationships, the feelings he'd had, the things he thought he'd learned. Rachel was asking her sister about future plans when they arrived back at the house.

"Philip's been talking to a group of surgeons in New York about joining their practice," Susan answered as they opened the front door. "He would have to give up most of his teaching, but he'd be doing reconstructive surgery exclusively, which is what he wants. He'd have more free time and a partnership in two years, if things work out."

"Sounds good." Rachel sniffed the air as they entered the house. "Something smells terrific."

The source of the inviting aroma was a guacamole omelet. Jason, who had discovered the recipe in one of Rachel's cookbooks, was sliding the first omelet onto a plate when the two women walked into the kitchen. Philip, looking like he'd just staggered out of bed, watched this operation with sleepy approval.

Susan dipped a finger into the bowl of guacamole, then informed Jason that if he ever tired of writing he was welcome to join their business as a junior partner.

Three more omelets joined the first and general conversation prevailed as everyone ate breakfast. Only after several cups of coffee was Philip sufficiently animated to drawl at Rachel, "Last night was tougher than a six-hour operation—at least the talking part of it was. Your sister's become one formidable lady in eighteen months. I guess it's better for both of us that way, even though it complicates my life."

He glanced at Susan and frowned. "But dammit, Suzy, if that punk surfer from California ever shows up in New York . . ." He let the sentence lapse, perhaps sensing that a threat of mayhem would turn the smile on Susan's face into gales of laughter.

"He wasn't a punk surfer," she said. "He was six foot, two, handsome and very smart. But I wasn't in love with him."

"So where do you go from here?" Jason asked.

Philip explained that he would be finished with his

job in Boston at the end of the month and then planned to join a group of New York plastic surgeons specializing in reconstructive surgery. "We're going to look for an apartment on the East Side. And Suzy is going to call Ellen Quinby to find out if she can see us. I know we'll need some help. I promised Suzy I would try to be responsive to both her and Ellen, and I will."

Given Philip's earlier refusal to seek professional counseling Rachel considered his willingness to see Dr. Quinby an important change in attitude. Though it was possible to go week after week with no resultant change in behavior, Philip seemed to realize that that would be a waste of his time and money.

"Have you considered setting a time limit?" Rachel asked aloud.

"Six months," Susan answered. "I don't expect miracles, but I won't wait indefinitely for some signs of progress."

"I wouldn't want you to," Philip said. "I know myself well enough to realize that I need some kind of deadline. Maybe part of the problem before was that Suzy was too patient. Although, frankly, eighteen months ago I didn't want to change. Now I think I do."

Jason grinned and shook his head at Philip's use of the qualifying word 'think,' prompting the latter to hold up his hand, laughing. "I *know* I do. Really!" he insisted.

They spent the rest of the morning reading the newspaper and doing the crossword puzzle, then broke for lunch. Afterward they played bridge for several hours. Susan had decided to stay in Boston with Philip until it was time to return to her New York commitments; the two of them left late that afternoon, dashing through the rain to the car, pausing to kiss before driving away.

Sunday night, Jason offered to put aside his work until Rachel left on Thursday morning, but she was far too sensitive to his mood to accept. She knew he was itching to get back to work and that his mind would be on his novel rather than on her during every minute of the proposed sightseeing and antiquing. At least they would have the evenings together, she thought.

She tried to keep busy with all her usual pursuits but found them more boring than ever. As the days passed she realized how deeply divided she was about leaving. As much as she hated to say good-bye to Jason she thought of the coming separation as temporary. Everything she had missed in New Hampshire was waiting for her in the city and she was eager to go back there.

The Labor Day picnic that Rachel and Susan had agreed to cater was the largest affair they had ever taken on—several hundred people would be present —and Rachel looked forward to the challenge. Almost all of the food could be prepared in advance, frozen and then re-heated, but because of the variety and amount involved they had allowed themselves three days to shop and cook. Had Rachel been home now she would probably have started work already.

It was Wednesday night before either she or Jason raised the subject of their future together. It had lain between them all week, the tension slowly growing until it was like a ghostly presence, joining their meals and conversations and sleeping in their bed at night.

As they lay together in the dark that night Jason reached over to stroke Rachel's hair. Normally that sort of affectionate gesture was a prelude to making love, but not on this occasion.

"I've told you what a good writer you are," he began. "Make it your career, Rachel. I know you're restless up here, but you wouldn't be spending every minute here. You'd be researching assignments, traveling around—I'd even come with you whenever I could."

"What about my business? September is half booked. We even have commitments for October."

"So meet them and then get out. Your sister will understand. She can find another partner."

That wasn't the point and both of them knew it. "I don't want her to find another partner. I love what we're doing. I wasn't cut out to be a full-time writer and I think you know that. It's not exciting enough for me."

"If you loved me you'd compromise. You'd live up here at least part of the time."

Rachel couldn't believe she was hearing this from Jason—understanding, empathetic, accomodating Jason. "Compromise?" she repeated. "How does that qualify as a compromise? You want me to give up a business I've worked years to establish to devote myself to a career that would bore me to distraction. I'd be miserable."

"We would have a family. Between that and writing . . ."

"A family? Really? And what would I do all day long, sing lullabies? There isn't another child within fifteen miles of this place, Jason. Maybe that suits *you*, but it isn't my idea of how to raise a family. Children need playmates." And mothers, she thought resentfully, need the company of other adults, even if their husbands don't.

Jason reached over and switched on the light. Only then did Rachel realize that his temper was just as inflamed as her own was. "If I'm so bloody neurotic," he said, "what are you doing up here with me? Hell, I'm amazed you haven't expired of terminal boredom by now."

"It's been a close call, believe me," Rachel snapped at him.

"So you're refusing to come up and see me, is that it?"

"I didn't say that," Rachel answered. "But now that you mention it, what would be the point? That's no relationship—a weekend or two every month. I don't see why you have to hide out up here like there's a contract on your life. You can write anywhere!"

"Can I?" Jason flung himself out of bed, stalked toward the hall and then returned to stand by the bed glaring down at Rachel. "What you mean by 'anywhere' is New York. Well, I don't know how you can stand it there!"

"It's exciting and interesting. Millions of people think so."

"Your 'millions of people' are developing lung cancer from air pollution. They have no woods to walk in or ride through. The snow turns to gray slush an hour after it falls and the traffic is impossible. Walk into a store and the salesman ignores you or yells at you." He paused. "Do I have to go on?"

Tired of lying there while Jason snarled down at her as if she were an unreasonable child, Rachel tossed back the covers, got out of bed and drew herself up to her full height. "So how did you survive L.A. *and* New York fifteen years ago?" she demanded.

"Things were more livable then and I was more resilient. I wasn't famous fifteen years ago. People weren't crawling all over me. But I'll tell you something, Rachel. I never enjoyed it. It was the best reason for doing films, especially if they were shooting on location. Why do you think I accepted *Parallel Universe?* Because I wanted to be a big star? Hell, it got me out of Los Angeles for a while! I live up here because I happen to like it."

"And that's that? Well, fine then! Enjoy your solitude. *I* won't be around to disturb it!"

She hadn't taken three steps before Jason caught her wrist to prevent her from going any farther. "All right, damn you, I'll move the house to the suburbs —Connecticut or Orange County. Will that satisfy you? We can be an hour from your precious city, but that's about the closest I can tolerate."

"And what am I supposed to do at one o'clock in the morning when I'm exhausted from a job? Get in the car and drive sixty miles to Fairfield County?"

"You can stay at your sister's."

"Five or six nights a week? You might as well live in Linwood!"

"Are you putting up roadblocks on purpose? Is that it?" Jason demanded. "I'm trying to find a compromise."

"Oh yes, you're very good at that!" Rachel knew she was being nasty, but she was confused and upset and no longer knew what she wanted. "I happen to like living in the city. My life there suits me. Why should I have to give it up just to be with you? And what would you be doing, anyway? Sitting in some room in front of a typewriter all day long!"

She yanked her wrist out of his grasp and ran out of the room. Minutes later, huddled under a comforter in one of the downstairs bedrooms, she brushed away a few self-righteous tears. Why should she have to give up the opera and the ballet and the theater? She wasn't cut out for suburban matronhood. If she didn't keep busy she started to feel restless. It wasn't as if she were asking Jason to keep her entertained. She only wanted him to live in New York so that she could keep *herself* entertained.

When he appeared in the doorway she tensed, telling herself that her point of view was entirely reasonable. After all, her work was in the city. He could write his blasted novels anywhere. If he needed to hole himself up somewhere, Central Park West was as good as Linwood, New Hampshire.

"Come back to bed, Rachel."

His tone was arrogant enough to stiffen the backbone of a slug. "I'm sleeping down here," she answered.

"Have it your way." He walked over to the bed, dropped his robe to the floor and started to climb in with her.

"Alone," she added.

"Like hell you are!" He reached for her with such an absence of gentleness that Rachel knew he was almost out of control. Her reaction was immediate. She twisted away from him, her heart pounding wildly, and ordered him to leave her alone.

Predictably enough, he paid no attention, straddling her body and pinning her hands above her head. Rachel remembered the last time she had been rendered helpless this way. It might have been a game *then*, but Jason was deadly serious *now*. Infuriated, she struggled until exhaustion forced her to stop. Then, having no other recourse, she glared up at him in motionless fury.

"Okay, you win." Jason sounded almost as out of breath as Rachel felt. "I'll finish the first draft of my novel. It will probably take me another two months. Then I'll come down to New York and stay with you and we'll see how things work out. Is that good enough?" He released her wrists and moved away from her to sit on the edge of the bed.

Rachel didn't understand why his capitulation failed to satisfy her. She had what she wanted, didn't she? He was staring at her, waiting for her answer, and after a short silence she answered, "Yes. All right."

"Just 'All right'? Not 'Great'? Or 'Terrific'? Or 'Thanks for being so understanding, Jason'?" he asked sarcastically. "You don't want to give an inch because that would mean commitment, which is exactly what this fight is all about. It isn't just a case of where we're going to live. It's whether we stay together."

"I suppose." It was humiliating, Rachel thought, to be with someone who understood your motivations sooner than you yourself did. Self-pity enveloped her. She loved Jason. Why was she so mixed up?

Without another word, he got up and walked out of the room.

After a few minutes of futile soul-searching Rachel followed. Although she felt guilty about her lack of sensitivity to Jason's point of view, if he was willing to come to New York, she would accept the offer. She would ask him to be patient with her. At the moment all she knew was that she couldn't bear to spend the night alone.

In fact, Jason asked no questions when he noticed Rachel standing in the doorway. Instead, he lifted the covers, silently inviting her to join him. His lovemaking was like their very first time together. Rachel felt the same desperate hunger, the same intense involvement. But this time her own emotions were equally engaged. Confused and distraught, she consciously sought the oblivion that wild arousal invariably brought her. For long minutes neither of them thought about anything other than the sensations elicited by their lovemaking, but no mere human could sustain that level of passion indefinitely. Their only weapon against their shared pain was the ability to re-experience that passionate oblivion time and again throughout the night.

Rachel resumed her life in New York with recharged fervor, behaving as though lack of activity were a dire moral failing. When she wasn't working or helping Susan look for an apartment she was visiting friends and catching up on culture. She even signed up for a weekly non-credit art course in spite of the fact that her schedule was so erratic that she would probably miss half of the classes.

Philip and Susan soon leased an East Side apartment convenient to his new office—a partner's wife had provided the necessary hot tip—and moved in during the third week in September. Until then, Philip had been Susan and Rachel's houseguest. Rather than feeling lonely when they left, Rachel was happy to have her own bed back and the bathroom to herself.

Her sister and brother-in-law were seeing Ellen Quinby once a week and both of them felt that the sessions were valuable. They provided a forum for airing grievances, with Dr. Quinby as a neutral referee. In addition, Philip was becoming more supportive of Susan's career and, although Susan would never be the stereotypical doctor's wife, she was willing to entertain his colleagues and join the appropriate committees. Most important to Susan, Philip was making an attempt to understand and share his feelings with her. He was genuinely trying to change and though his progress was something short of dazzling Susan was encouraged about their future together.

Rachel's relationship with Jason resulted in one immediate change in her life: she was now included in the social circle she had formerly served as a caterer. Paula Chapin called her two days after she returned to New York to invite her to a dinner party—the first of many such invitations. Rachel soon accustomed herself to the fact that one night she might be sitting in the dining room eating dinner and two nights later standing at the stove cooking it. Now, however, some of the guests could usually be found hanging around the kitchen, talking to her and Susan while they worked, and they invariably ended their evenings in the living room with everyone else. In spite of a need to fend off questions about Jason, Rachel enjoyed the attention she received. Her new acquaintances were bright and witty and she felt a sense of importance in their company.

She spoke to Jason every few nights. After each conversation she realized that she missed him, but she was much too tired from running around all day for loneliness to keep her awake at night. As for Jason, he was thoroughly absorbed in his novel and apparently spent every waking moment on it. Rachel handled her occasional pangs of depression by reminding herself that Jason would be coming to New York at the end of October. Everything would be perfect . . . then.

Susan's reconciliation with Philip led to a second change in Rachel's life. One of the first things that Dr. Quinby pointed out was that, with Philip working days and Susan working most evenings, they had very little time to be together. As a consequence, Rachel and Susan agreed to limit the number of dinners they catered to two or three a week, a policy that took effect by the beginning of October. They also decided to diversify, looking for work in fields allied with the catering business but with more acceptable hours, such as Rachel's free-lance writing.

A recommendation from Harry Pollock to a friend who was directing a T.V. movie on location in Manhattan resulted in an assignment to prepare a five-course French dinner—for the cameras. As the more artistic sister, Susan particularly enjoyed the challenge of creating food that not only looked beautiful but stayed beautiful, sometimes for hours at a time. It didn't faze her that wilting salads and congealed sauces frequently had to be replaced with fresh clones.

After two similar jobs—one a television commercial, the other a magazine layout—their reputation started to spread. Rachel supposed that eventually they would eliminate almost all dinner parties, but she was prepared for that. She was already filling her newly-freed evenings with lectures, socializing and magazine projects; she would simply add another course or two.

She realized that her energy level was decreasing, of course, but bridled at the notion of slowing down. After all, there was no great mystery as to the cause of her fatigue. Rachel was pregnant and told herself that she was thrilled about it. At times she marveled at her own unconventionality. She had been such a little conformist at twenty and here she was, twenty-eight, unmarried and looking forward to motherhood. Although she had never in fact had a problem she had believed herself infertile for so many years that the baby seemed like a biological miracle to her. She hadn't been daring enough to plan this pregnancy, but had done nothing to prevent it. On an unconscious level that was surely intentional. Having the child of a man she loved would have provided deep satisfaction to Rachel under any circumstances, but the fact that Jason had always wanted children made her pregnancy even more special.

Only one thing kept her from sharing it with him. She wanted to find out whether they could be happy together in New York before she agreed to marry him. She didn't want to pressure him into a decision. Though they had never resolved their argument in New Hampshire Rachel was honest enough to admit to herself that Jason was right. She wanted it all: the baby, Jason *and* her current lifestyle. And there was no good reason, beyond Jason's pathological dislike of the city, why she couldn't have it.

After almost a week of silence Jason phoned the last Thursday evening in October to tell Rachel that he had finished the first draft of his novel and would be flying to New York the next day. He asked her to pick him up at the airport, but since she and Susan had a luncheon to cater, they agreed to meet at her apartment at three.

Rachel told herself that if Jason would only give her lifestyle a chance he would come to like it. They would be doing interesting, enjoyable things together after all. Paula and Stephen had asked her to dinner on Saturday and she would pick up off-Broadway matinee tickets for Sunday. She and Susan had a cocktail party to cater on Monday and she could ask friends in on Tuesday. Jason had mentioned lunch with his publisher; they would have to fit that in sometime early in the week.

She sailed through most of Friday, managing to get back to her apartment ten minutes early. Jason was standing and talking to the doorman, oblivious to the stares of passersby, only acknowledging the people who stopped and asked for autographs. Rachel flew out of the taxi and into his arms, their kiss the beginning of a blissful reunion. They made love, cooked dinner together and then made love again. It was the best night's sleep Rachel had had in two months.

Saturday was going to be one of those perfect October days, Rachel thought the next morning as she looked out the window: sweet and clear, the warmth of the sun taking the bite out of the nippy fall air.

She fixed breakfast in bed for two, then curled up next to Jason while they ate. "It's beautiful outside," she said. "You can't complain about pollution today, Jason. Let's walk around the city. You can take me shopping for a teddy to replace the one you demolished and then we'll go picnic in the park."

"You're wound up like a corkscrew," he answered. "Why don't we stay around your apartment and relax? We've hardly talked. We can leave the window open if you need atmosphere."

Rachel remembered that Jason had been working very hard for the last few weeks and immediately gave in. They talked about Philip and Susan and then about plans for the week, but by eleven o'clock Rachel was so restless that Jason agreed to take her shopping.

They went into three different department stores before she found something she liked, with the same scene endlessly repeating itself: a stare, a double take, a request for an autograph, tiresome questions. Rachel had expected these intrusions and reacted with either charm or coolness, as the occasion demanded. And, she decided, Jason was coping quite well. He had perfected the smiling dismissal into a foolproof weapon.

They skipped the picnic in favor of a hasty push-cart hot dog, then took a taxi back to Rachel's apartment. Jason had a number of calls to make and while he was on the phone Rachel started to read his manuscript. Like his first two books, it was tightly written, graphic and compelling. She put it down only because it was time to dress for the Chapins' dinner party.

Thinking about it later that night, she was certain

that Jason had enjoyed himself. He preferred small gatherings such as this one and most of those present were friends of his. For once in his life Stephen was on his best behavior and had enough common sense not to raise the subject of his play. On the whole, Rachel thought afterward, their first day and a half had been a success.

The next few days were even better. Susan and Philip joined them for the Sunday matinee followed by dinner in a Chinatown restaurant and Rachel was relieved to see that Jason handled the celebrity-watchers with greater ease than ever before. On Monday Jason's publisher invited them for lunch in the company's executive dining room. His agent and editor were also present and, although it was the publisher who raised the subject of publicity, within minutes all three men were urging Jason to agree to a television interview while in New York. He had introduced Rachel only by her maiden name, yet all of them seemed to know exactly who she was, a tribute to New York's literary grapevine.

Although Rachel didn't say so aloud she took the position that Jason was a public person and that the sooner he accepted that fact the healthier it would be for him. She was so convinced of these things that she took the once unthinkable step of offering to appear on television with him to talk about *A Latin American Tragedy*.

He argued halfheartedly for ten minutes, then gave in, stipulating only that he preferred non-commercial television and specified a well-known interviewer who taped his shows locally. Rachel found out that people were willing to rearrange their schedules for a fish of Jason Wilder's size and elusiveness. The taping, for two consecutive half-hour shows, was scheduled for Thursday.

The cocktail party that Susan and Rachel had contracted to cater that night was in honor of a New England painter who was having his first major show in New York. Later, Rachel was sorry that she had coaxed Jason into coming. The artist was temperamental and egotistical and made no effort to hide his fury when he was upstaged by what he called a "pulp writer." He conveniently ignored the fact that Jason's presence meant valuable publicity for himself. The painter's temper tantrum was featured prominently in the next day's papers.

On Tuesday Rachel catered a brunch for thirty-five and then had friends in for dinner; on Wednesday she and Jason took in a second matinee, went home for a few hours and then met a different group of friends at an "in" East Side restaurant. As for the T.V. session on Thursday, nobody could have asked for a more generous, easy-going interviewer. Even Rachel, who had initially been nervous, soon relaxed and enjoyed herself.

She and Susan had a television commercial to do early Friday morning so she was up and out of the apartment even before Jason woke up. They wrapped up the ad early in the afternoon and Rachel immediately started to think about the coming weekend. They had a dinner party to cater that would take up all of Saturday, but Sunday was open. Perhaps she and Jason could ask some friends to join them for a ride upstate, if the weather cooperated.

She walked into the apartment to find Jason sitting on the couch, his two suitcases on the floor by his feet. Since the week had been near-perfect as far as Rachel was concerned she immediately assumed that a problem had come up. "What's the matter?" she asked. "It isn't your mother, is it?"

As soon as the words were out Jason's expression registered on Rachel's consciousness. He wasn't angry or upset—defeated and withdrawn came closer to the truth.

"It's not going to work," he told her. "For the last week I've been trying to live the way you want me to—and I've hated almost all of it. As much as I—"

"How can you say that?" Rachel interrupted. She walked further into the room until she was standing about two yards away from him, staring down at him in stupefaction. "You were enjoying yourself. You didn't even mind the fans."

"I was enjoying myself maybe a third of the time, and I *did* mind the fans. You were too busy putting your *own* interpretation on things to notice how *I* felt." He stood up. "You know something, Rachel? I had to see you in New York to understand how frenetic you really are. This city seems to hype you up. You have the right to choose how you want to live, but don't expect me to share it with you."

Rachel asked herself how she could have misjudged his mood so totally, then answered her own question. He'd been putting on an act! "Why didn't you tell me how you felt," she lashed out, "instead of pretending that everything was terrific? Am I supposed to be a mind-reader? I thought you were so hot on honesty!"

He frowned impatiently. "I was trying to do things the way you wanted. I was *honestly* trying to like it.

But it didn't work. Face facts, Rachel. We're too different to live together. Now I can see why living in the suburbs would be hopeless. Without your daily fix of ballet, opera, theater, parties . . ." His voice trailed off. "I'm going back to New Hampshire."

Rachel felt betrayed, abandoned. How could he do this to her? "Just like that? I thought you loved me so much!"

Her accusation demolished what little restraint Jason had left. "You want the truth? Okay, then! I've seen some things in New York I didn't see in New Hampshire. You aren't all that different from Maria. You're just a slightly older extension of her. You still spend sixteen hours a day chasing around after who-knows-what, only now work is part of the package so that makes you liberated. You like all the chic restaurants and being with the right people, and I don't give a damn about those things. If that isn't Maria—the 'in' crowd, the 'in' places—you tell me what is. Do you realize that the only times we've been able to enjoy each other this week were in bed? Probably the only reason you let me get close to you in New Hampshire was because you knew it would have to end. You want the bottom line, Rachel? I need someone to be with, to talk to, to build something with. You're not my idea of a wife, sweetheart, and you're *certainly* not my idea of a mother!"

Rachel was so incensed by these observations that she picked up one of Jason's suitcases and flung it toward the door. "Go back to your safe little world in New Hampshire, then!" she yelled. "Marry some long-haired mother who'll sit in a rocking chair nursing babies all day. She'll be just about your speed!"

Jason simply shook his head, picked up the second suitcase and retrieved the one that had caromed off the wall. Then he let himself out of the apartment.

# Chapter Twelve

At first Rachel told herself that she was lucky to be rid of him. Her only mistake had been in thinking that a summer fling had been eternal love. Only a fool would miss a man who could lash into her as viciously as Jason had during their final, vicious argument.

But as much as she tried to dismiss his accusations, they haunted her. Was she really so superficial? *Was* her behavior in Santandia analogous to her behavior in New York, the only difference being the substitution of more praiseworthy pursuits? Was constant activity a way of avoiding relationships, commitments? After a week of righteous indignation Rachel began to consider the possibility that Jason was right about her. He always had been so far.

Even so, she didn't know what to do about it. Whenever she wasn't busy she started to get depressed. She accelerated the pace of her life to such an extent that there was little time left to think or feel and brushed off Susan's warning that she was risking both her own health and that of the child.

It took until the beginning of December for Rachel to acknowledge that her method of coping with the split from Jason was doing her absolutely no good. Her nights were restless and her appetite was lousy. She'd been running herself ragged for a solid month and the only result was exhaustion. The truth of the matter was that she had neither the desire nor the energy to go out every night.

She started to spend more time with Susan, finally admitting what her sister had already guessed: what Rachel had explained away as an unimportant lover's quarrel was in fact far more serious. She forced herself to confront another major problem: although she wanted her child and would never have considered terminating the pregnancy, she was frightened by the idea of being alone. She had always assumed that Jason would share the day-to-day responsibilities of parenthood, but now it seemed that the major burden would be on her. She couldn't earn a living, flit around the city *and* call herself a decent mother. Unless she wanted to relinquish the care of her child to a housekeeper she had to make some changes in her life.

To her surprise, the thought was a relief. She told Susan that pregnancy had mellowed her, but, no matter what the cause, she began to find that a quiet evening with Susan and Philip held more appeal than a raucous, smoke-filled party. Some instinct finally led her to seek out the people who truly cared about her. They didn't so much cheer her up as provide solace.

A week and a half before Christmas Paula Chapin

called, saying that she had missed Rachel at a recent party and was inviting her and Jason to dinner on Saturday night. "He sent Stephen a note saying that he was coming into town," she explained. "We'll keep it small. Just two other couples besides the four of us."

Paula obviously had no idea what had happened, so it was easier to tell her the truth rather than hedge. "Jason and I aren't together anymore," Rachel said. "But thanks for asking me, Paula."

Paula Chapin was much too tactful to ask for details. She said that she was sorry and that she hoped that Rachel would come to dinner some other time, when Jason wasn't present.

Only after that weekend did Rachel finally permit herself to give in to the pain she had thus far refused to feel. She had stayed in the apartment during every non-working hour, waiting for the phone to ring or the doorbell to buzz. Both had been silent. The knowledge that Jason had come to New York and hadn't wanted to see her was devastating. She spent Monday in bed, not eating, just crying and staring at the ceiling. Christmastime was a busy season for her and Susan, so it wasn't possible to carry on that way day after day, but Rachel wanted to. At first only the memory of her earlier experiences kept her going. She'd survived a hell of a lot more than a broken romance in her time, hadn't she?

She thought about calling Jason, but couldn't bring herself to do so. If she told him that she loved him and offered to live with him in Connecticut, and then he refused, she would have to accept the break-up as final. She couldn't face that just yet. She needed to be able to hope.

Christmas with her family brought her one step closer to making that phone call. It had been years since Thomas and Helena Grant had been able to join their daughters in New York, but this year they came because Susan told them that Rachel needed to see them. It wasn't easy for Rachel to tell her parents about the mess she had landed herself in, especially in view of her disastrous marriage, but they couldn't have been more wonderful. Their only criticism was that Rachel hadn't told Jason about the child, but when she explained that she refused to pressure him into a marriage he might not want anymore they understood her point of view.

On the last day of their visit they invited Rachel to make her home with them in Tokyo, but five days of familial love and support had helped her to regain the equilibrium that had become such an innate part of her character. She wasn't the first single parent in the world and she wouldn't be the last. In fact, she was far more fortunate than most; she knew that Jason would meet his financial obligations. Knowing him, he would also help raise the child.

Rachel stopped reacting to things and started to take control of her life again. She was less tired and more settled now. The future, though frightening and lonely, finally held the promise of joy, as well. When she felt the baby move inside her she would smile, and even though the smile was a wistful one, there was far more happiness than pain in it. She had come to understand what commitment meant. It was choosing to share your life with someone even though you knew you could make it without him. It was a desire to work out problems through compromise instead of insisting on your own way. She only hoped that Jason would listen when she told him that she was ready to do those things. The telephone was such a cold method of communication that she thought about writing to him, asking him to come see her. And it would have to be soon, before her pregnancy became obvious.

She was finishing up the Sunday paper on the second Monday in January when she noticed an advertisement in the Arts section that made her go pale. "Harold L. Pollock presents Stephen Chapin's *Power Play*," it read. The stars were listed side by side below the title—and Jason Wilder was one of them. The opening date was early March, with the first preview some two weeks before.

Rachel wondered if Jason had changed his mind about doing the play because she was in New York, because he wanted to be with her. She knew that there was no logical reason to think so, given the verbal flailing she'd received, but she wanted to believe it and therefore she did.

She picked up the phone before she could talk herself out of it and punched the Chapins' number. When Stephen answered the phone she began rather breathlessly, "It's Rachel. I saw the ad in the paper. I wondered when Jason was coming to New York, because I want to speak to him."

"How are you doing? Why don't we see you anymore? Are you hibernating?" Question followed question with no pauses in between.

"No, of course not. I've been fine," Rachel answered. Then she admitted, "Well, surviving might be more honest, but I'll be okay. When . . ."

"He's here now. He's staying with me and Paula, and he's *not* so okay, Rachel. I don't know what made him change his mind about doing the play, but

244

whatever it was, he won't talk about it. Just a minute—I'll get him."

Requesting the date of Jason's arrival hadn't been easy for Rachel and the prospect of talking to him was even worse. Though she found Stephen's words encouraging, by the time she heard Jason's curt, "Yes?" her heart was thudding doubletime and her face felt flushed.

"It's Rachel," she said. Oh, no, she thought, he already *knows* that. Just get to the point! "I wanted to talk to you. Would you like to come—for lunch?"

"I'm busy for lunch. I could stop by your apartment on my way downtown if it's important."

His tone was somewhere between distant and hostile. Rachel almost told him to forget it, but the strong side of her—the side that was ready to make her pitch and wait for judgement—won out. "I'll be here," she said softly and hung up the phone.

As she showered and dressed she rehearsed what she would say. She really felt different now. Two painful months had finally shown her what she wanted. She would make Jason understand that. Her pregnancy had only recently forced her out of her everyday clothing and she quite deliberately put on a loosely belted jumper that revealed nothing. Jason had to want *her*, not her and the baby.

When the doorbell rang Rachel was pacing around the living room, wondering why a ten minute trip was taking Jason more than three times that long. Jason's blank expression aborted her instinct to smile as she opened the door. "Come in," she murmured. "Can I get you a cup of coffee?"

He seemed impatient with this pretence of normalcy. "My lunch date is at noon. Will this take more than half an hour?"

Rachel shook her head and gestured toward the sofa, not understanding why he was making this difficult for her. He had to know what she was going to say. Why else would she have asked him to come?

"I've been doing a lot of thinking the last few months," she began. Unable to sit or stand still, she was wandering aimlessly around the room as she talked. "I was hurt by what you said when you left, and angry, but I know there was a lot of truth in it. All that activity *was* a way of running away from personal commitments. I suppose I only let myself fall in love with you because you lived in New Hampshire and it felt safe to me. But I really don't see myself as a social butterfly anymore, Jason. Your friends are very glamorous, and maybe I got carried away, but it was only temporary. I think I've settled down and learned what's important. I hardly ever go out anymore."

She glanced up to judge his reaction. His expression was unreadable—poker-faced. Sensing that he was becoming impatient, she decided to leave out the blow-by-blow description of her daily regimen. "I love you and I want us to work things out. I won't pretend that I can be happy in New Hampshire, but if you're still willing to live in Connecticut I'd like to do that."

So much for the speech, she thought. Jason had no visible response to it, other than to glance at his watch. "Is that all you have to say?" he asked.

In almost twenty-nine years of living Rachel had never experienced anything like the pain his question caused her. It was as though somebody had stabbed her and twisted the knife, very slowly and very deliberately. For several long moments she was too close to tears to talk and then somehow she got a grip on her emotions and knew that the crying would come later, when she was alone. She wasn't going to beg for a man who no longer wanted her. She was strong and capable and she could make it on her own.

She had one more item of business to deal with and putting it off wouldn't make it any easier. Settle it now, she thought. Make an end to it.

"No, there's something else." Her voice was husky but firm. She was standing still now, in pain, but also in control. She didn't mince words. "I'm pregnant. The baby is due at the end of May. I just want you to know that I'm going to be a good mother, Jason. I want this child and I'm not going to run around while some other woman raises it."

You're getting off the track, she told herself. He doesn't care about how devoted you're going to be. Just stick to the facts. "I plan to nurse the baby, so for the first six or eight months, I'll have to stay with her—or him. But you can come and see her whenever you want to or I'll come to New Hampshire, if that would be easier. After that, we'll have to work something out. I understand that the child is half yours and that you want her as much as I do. So maybe when she's old enough we can alternate months, because I've been reading a lot and children —children are very resilient. They adapt, as long as there's love . . ."

"Rachel, you don't have to . . ." Jason began.

"No, let me finish," Rachel interrupted. And stop being maudlin, she scolded herself. Talk to him about money. "I'll need some help with the medical bills. My insurance is only minimal for childbirth."

Rachel was looking in Jason's direction, but no longer seeing him. The minute she had mentioned childbirth she had stepped into a world of her own, wrapped herself up in a cocoon of fear and pain. She had never been in a hospital, except for tests on an outpatient basis. Her body was not well-suited to childbearing, and her doctor had mentioned the possibility of a Caesarian section, although he hoped it wouldn't be necessary.

She hated herself for what she was about to say, but knew she would say it anyway. "Difficult deliveries run in my family," she continued, repeating what her mother had gently told her. "The doctor says I'm very narrow, Jason, and, well, it would mean a lot to me if you would be there with me, if you can. I mean, if you don't mind about the publicity. Besides, there are theories about infant/parent bonding . . . they say if you hold your baby right away . . ."

If she said one more word, she was going to crack. She was somewhere between throwing up and bursting into tears when she looked down at Jason. The pain and guilt she saw in his eyes reminded her that she still had a backbone. "I don't want your pity, damn you!" she snapped, starting to cry.

He murmured her name, shaking his head, and then stood up, turning his back to her. "I thought I'd make it easier for you to kick me exactly where I deserve it," he said.

Rachel stood rooted to the floor, too overwrought to interpret his comment. After a long five seconds he seemed to realize that she had no intention of kicking him anywhere and turned around.

"Do you think you'll be happy in Connecticut?" he asked her.

"I'm not going to let you marry me just because I happen to be pregnant," Rachel insisted, rubbing the tears from her eyes.

"Does the fact that we love each other qualify as a reason?"

"You didn't call me the last time you were in New York," she reminded him, "and when you came in here today it seemed like you could hardly wait to leave. Now you want to marry me. Why?"

"Will you let me hold you while I explain?"

It was such a soulful plea that Rachel softened, walking into his arms, returning his hug, half-grateful and half-disappointed when he made no attempt to deepen his gentle kiss into a passionate one. They sat down on the couch, Jason coaxing Rachel's head onto his shoulder.

"I went into this relationship with my eyes open," he said. "I probably had no right to give you a sermon when none of the problems were new ones. But I was frustrated and out of patience. I thought it might do some good."

"I wasn't ready to listen," Rachel admitted. "Not until you came down here and didn't even call me."

"There was no point to it. I couldn't live in a city I disliked with a wife I never saw. The next move, if there was a next move, had to come from you."

"And today? Why were you so. . . ." She interrupted herself to make the astonished observation that Jason was blushing.

"I'm embarrassed. My only defense is that I was lonely and angry with you and not thinking rationally. When your sister wrote me to tell me you were pregnant all I could think of was the way Meredith had acted."

"Suzy wrote you?" Rachel asked. Her sister had changed more than she had realized.

"She felt I should know. She was upset that you hadn't told me yet. She thought it would help to have things resolved. And I immediately jumped to the conclusion that you weren't telling me because you didn't want me to have anything to do with the baby—that you were going to punish me for leaving you by withholding my child from me. Five minutes after I read the letter I called Harry Pollock, told him I was going to do the play and made arrangements to come to New York. I got here last night. I had no real idea why I had come or what I was going to do here, but when you called me up and asked me to come over I assumed it was to talk about the baby. And when you didn't bring it up right away I decided my initial feelings had been right."

"I didn't want to pressure you," Rachel said. "I would have written you asking you to come down— probably in another week or two."

"Obviously. I was too twisted up inside to remember that the woman I loved had more guts and morality than I probably deserve. Forgive me?"

How could the world change so quickly? Rachel wondered. She was becoming euphoric from it, giggly. "If you want to stand up now," she teased, "I'll give you that kick you wanted."

Instead, he brushed her hair away from the neckline of her jumper, unzipped it and began to unfasten the buttons down the back of her blouse. "I can think of better things to do. Like looking at my child."

After dispensing with the last button he unhooked her bra, commenting, "What's the point of this? I didn't know you even owned one."

Lazing back against the cushions of the sofa, Rachel invited, "Why don't you feel for yourself?"

Jason slipped the jumper down to her waist and removed the blouse, then pushed aside her bra to caress her breasts. They had become increasingly fuller as her pregnancy progressed. "Very nice," he murmured. His hand wandered lower, feeling the firm curve of her abdomen. Rachel caressed his cheek and then guided his head to her mouth, well satisfied by how quickly his kiss deepened from tenderness to hungry passion. His tongue stopped its restless probing only reluctantly, his lips traveling to her ear to whisper, "You're sure this is all right?"

"As long as we're careful about it," Rachel murmured, starting to undress him. She was working on the middle button of his shirt when he picked her up and carried her into the bedroom.

"Jason, that lunch appointment . . ." she said.

"It's nobody important—just some T.V. interviewer I promised to meet." He set her on the bed, finished undressing her and then removed his clothing with a deliberation meant to tease. His lovemaking was gently passionate and although Rachel felt like a witch for touching him in a way that tested his self-control she kept on doing so because it was obvious that he loved every minute of it.

Afterward they lay in each other's arms and talked about the future. Jason had agreed to a two-month run in Stephen's play and admitted he had probably allowed Rachel's pregnancy to spur him into a commitment only because, fundamentally, he wanted to act again and because he had assumed that they would be together, at least temporarily.

"But if you don't take good care of me," he threatened, "I'll never survive New York till May. I thought we could buy a piece of land and move the house there. We'll need a finished basement for the kids. It will probably take . . ."

Rachel stopped him. "Wait a minute," she said. "Was that *kids*, as in 'more than one'?"

"Sure. I figure that if I keep you barefoot and pregnant you won't turn hyper on me," he teased.

Only then did Rachel tell him of an idea she had barely acknowledged, even to herself. "As a matter of fact, Philip and Susan are doing really well and they've been talking about leaving the city, maybe even having a child. There's a store I've been to, a combination lunch place and gourmet take-out, and I was thinking that maybe the two of us could start something similar. We'd still be doing . . ." She interrupted herself after noticing the time. "Jason, it's almost noon. Even though the person you were meeting isn't a bigshot, shouldn't you call him up and tell him you'll be late?"

*"We'll* be late," he amended. "Somehow or other I let Harry Pollock talk me into this. It was probably that line of yours about my 'safe little world' in New Hampshire, so you can damn well come along." He picked up the phone, punched a number and then waited for a few moments. "Jason Wilder calling. I'll hold." He turned back to Rachel and grinned. "I figured if I'm going to rejoin civilization I might as well do it on prime time network T.V."

# *If you enjoyed this book...*

...you will enjoy a Special Edition Book Club membership even more.

It will bring you each new title, as soon as it is published every month, delivered right to your door.

### 15-Day Free Trial Offer

We will send you 6 new Silhouette Special Editions to keep for 15 days absolutely free! If you decide not to keep them, send them back to us, you pay nothing. But if you enjoy them as much as we think you will, keep them and pay the invoice enclosed with your trial shipment. You will then automatically become a member of the Special Edition Book Club and receive 6 more romances every month. There is no minimum number of books to buy and you can cancel at any time.

*Silhouette Special Edition*

## Coming Next Month

### Silver Mist by Sondra Stanford

Laurel Patterson ran away with her sister and niece to a small town in Texas to escape from a disastrous love affair. To finally free her mind from the painful memories, Laurel concentrates all her energy on setting up the child-care center she and her sister are starting. Then Stephen Tanner, a local rancher, enters her world and proceeds to win over her sister and niece. Laurel slowly and unwillingly succumbs to his charms and irresistible manner. But now that Laurel has adjusted to the challenge of a new life and a new business, the hardest challenge of all is adjusting to a new man.

### Texas Rose by Katharine Thiels

Alexis Kellogg's big breakthrough as a reporter brought her back to the town she had left in scandal—and into the arms of the man who drove her away. Cade Morse was one of the richest men in Texas and Alexis' job was to discover what drove him to the top. Was her destiny in his arms . . . or in the truth she was sent to unearth, the article she was compelled to write?

### Never Give Your Heart by Tracy Sinclair

Gillian North was thrilled to land the Bliss Cosmetics account, but not with Bliss owner, Roman Barclay, who was determined to make Gillian part of the deal.

Then, quickly, things changed between them, and Gillian began to dream of a shared future. But the dream was shattered when Roman showed, unmistakably, just what she was to him: a prize possession, expensively bought.

She knew her heart was lost; could she salvage her pride?

## Silhouette Special Edition

## Coming Next Month

### Keys To Daniel's House by Carole Halston

Sydney Cullen had no use for men. All her energies went into her family and her career. The accusation that her looks were behind her success stung, and she grasped the chance to disprove the statement.

How could she have known that in using Daniel Bates to prove her point she would prove only that, no matter how hard she tried, she could never escape her own needs, her own passions?

### All Our Tomorrows by Mary Lynn Baxter

Ex-tennis star Brooke Lawson's brother insists she recover from her crippling car accident at his home in Hawaii. Faced with the possible end to her career, Brooke struggles to regain her confidence and physical strength amidst her tormenting attraction to entrepreneur, Ashley Graham. Ashley, a hard-driving and virile man, arranges a marriage with her which she must accept to learn the depth of her passion for him. But can she continue a forced commitment to a man who demands all of her?

### Love Is Surrender by Carolyn Thornton

Jennifer Waring, an attractive, young journalist, heartbroken over her divorce, felt like she belonged to another era as she drove down the treelined drive to the Esplanade plantation. She had been hired to publicize Esplanade and its owner, Ham Bertout. Ham relights the flame of desire within Jennifer, as she does in him. It is Jennifer's desire to do what is right and to be certain her love for her ex-husband is over that nearly destroys their new found love.

# MORE ROMANCE FOR
# A SPECIAL WAY TO RELAX